Grammar 5

Answer Guide and Resources

Edited by Amber Densmer

Show me your ways, O LORD,
teach me your paths.

Psalm 25:4 (NIV)

SONLIGHT
The way you wish you'd been taught.

Sonlight Curriculum® "Grammar 5" Answer Guide and Resources, First Edition

Copyright © 2010 by Sonlight Curriculum, Ltd.

"Do to others what you would have them do to you" (Matthew 7:12).

"The worker is worth his keep" (Matthew 10:10).

Published by
Sonlight Curriculum, Ltd.
8042 South Grant Way
Littleton, CO 80122-2705
USA
Phone (303) 730-6292   Fax (303) 795-8668
E-mail: main@sonlight.com

NOTE TO PURCHASER

Sonlight Curriculum, Ltd. is committed to providing the best homeschool resources on the market. This entails regular upgrades to our curriculum and to our Instructor's Guides. This guide is the 2010 Edition of the Sonlight Curriculum® Grammar 5 Answer Guide and Resources. If you purchased it from a source other than Sonlight Curriculum, Ltd., you should know that it may not be the latest edition available.

This guide is sold with the understanding that none of the Authors nor the Publisher is engaged in rendering educational services. Questions relevant to the specific educational or legal needs of the user should be addressed to practicing members of those professions.

The information, ideas, and suggestions contained herein have been developed from sources, including publications and research, that are considered and believed to be reliable but cannot be guaranteed insofar as they apply to any particular classroom or homeschooling situation.

The Authors and Publisher specifically disclaim any liability, loss, or risk, personal or otherwise, incurred as a consequence directly or indirectly of the use and application of any of the suggestions or contents of this guide.

Printed in the United States of America.

For the latest information about changes in this guide, please visit **www.sonlight.com/curriculum-updates.html** 🖥. Please notify us of any errors you find not listed on this site. E-mail corrections to *IGcorrections@sonlight.com* and any suggestions you may have to *IGsuggestions@sonlight.com*.

Table of Contents

Section One: Introduction to This Program

Section Two: Answer Guide

Grammar 5 Answer Guide

Section Three: Resources

This page intentionally left blank.

Grammar 5 Introduction

Welcome

In this program, your family will dig deeper into cracking the grammatical code that creates the foundation and structure of our language. This program provides grammatical practice made practical—we teach grammar directly from materials your children read, and help them apply it back to their writing.

Included in this Program

Grammar 5 Answer Guide

The **Answer Guide**, found directly after this page, provides instructional information for and answers to the Activity Sheet exercises. The Answer Guide usually contains the same information as your children's Activity Sheets, though at times we have summarized the main points of the instructional **F.Y.I.** section as an **F.Y.I. Synopsis** in the Answer Guide.

Grammar 5 Activity Sheets

This program meets your children on familiar ground. The separate book of **Activity Sheets** use passages from age-appropriate books as the backdrop to the grammatical skills we teach each day.

Passages

Every Activity Sheet opens with a **Passage** from a great book written at the reading level appropriate for a Sonlight Level 5 student. While these passages may come from books your children read, they do not align to any reading schedule in any of our other Sonlight Instructor's Guides.

Grammatical Instruction

Some Activity Sheets contain an **F.Y.I.** section that formally introduces a grammatical topic or concept used in the Activity Sheet exercises. The **F.Y.I. Synopsis** in the Answer Guide summarizes the main points of the Activity Sheet's F.Y.I.

When a passage provides the opportunity for a bonus grammar lesson, we will occasionally introduce a topic in the beginning of a question.

Exercises

Your children then practice these grammar concepts we've taught through the Activity Sheet **Exercises**. Do not feel obligated to complete every question on every Activity Sheet. Feel free to adjust and/or omit activities to meet the needs of your children. We cover the same concepts repeatedly throughout the year to enable your children to learn "naturally" through repetition and practice over time.

Resources

The final portion of this program is a **Resource** section that contains two handy tools. The first is a **List of Standard Symbols**, which is a key to the abbreviations we ask your children to use as they mark up the daily passages. The List of Standard Symbols is also located in the front of your child's Activity Sheet book for easy reference. The second is the **Grammar Guide**—a concise resource that contains explanations of grammatical topics and examples.

We use various symbols on the **Skills Matrix** to show when we both present and practice topics throughout the year. Please find the Skills Matrix toward the end of the Resource section for more information.

How to Schedule this Program

This program contains 72 Activity Sheets—enough for you to complete two Activity Sheets per week for a 36 week school year.

How to Begin

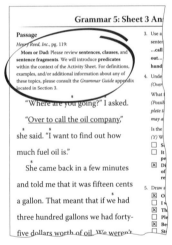

Before you begin each day, please check the **Mom or Dad:** section of the Answer Guide notes to make sure we haven't asked you to introduce a grammatical topic on your own. If we have, please review the brief instruction and examples we provide in the *Grammar Guide* in the Resource section with your children before they begin the Activity Sheet.

If the Activity Sheet contains an **F.Y.I.** section of instruction, you may want to read through it with your children to better answer any questions they may have.

Sonlight's *Language Arts 5* Users

To use with the Sonlight *Language Arts 5* program, choose one of the options below:

Complete these Activity Sheets in place of the *Grammar Ace* assignments scheduled each week.

—OR—

Use these Activity Sheets on Day 2 and Day 4 each week.

Grammar 5 Introduction

—OR—

Use the dictation passage from the regular *Language Arts 5* activity sheet on Day 1, then complete the *Grammar 5* Activity Sheet afterwards. Add the second *Grammar 5* Activity Sheet as it best fits your schedule on Days 2-5. **Note:** We deliberately do not link the dictation assignments in this program to the books you read.

Dictation

If you plan to pair these Activity Sheets with our *Language Arts 5* program, we recommend you use the passage included in the Language Arts Instructor's Guide as they correspond with your children's weekly reading assignments.

However, if you would like your children to have more interaction with the text they will use for grammatical analysis, use the passages on the Grammar 5 Activity Sheets instead for the dictation portion of your Language Arts instruction. You may find that your children have an easier time picking the passages apart if they've had a little time to hear and read through them prior to working on the Grammar Activity Sheets.

So Why Learn Grammar Anyway?

Our language is a code—seemingly arbitrary sounds are fitted together into words, sentences and paragraphs. When we learn grammar, we learn how those pieces of sounds and words fit together and interact with one another. We begin to see how those elements work together in the language we write and speak daily. We learn to decipher the code, and we improve as writers because of it.

We found a comment in A. W. Tozer's *The Size of the Soul: Principles of Revival and Spiritual Growth* that we thought put the study of Language Arts in an eternal light. Hopefully your children will find these thoughts helpful the next time they appear to need a reason to excel at Language Arts:

> For the very reason that God has committed His saving truth to the receptacle of human language, the man who preaches that truth should be more than ordinarily skillful in the use of language. It is necessary that every artist master his medium, every musician his instrument. For a man calling himself a concert pianist to appear before an audience with but a beginner's acquaintance with the keyboard would be no more absurd than for a minister of the gospel to appear before his congregation without a thorough knowledge of the language in which he expects to preach. [pp. 41-42]

In other words, those of us who want to share God's eternal truths should be more than ordinarily skillful in the use of the language in which we want to communicate.

Tozer's thoughts on mastering the medium of language were echoed by John Piper in an article titled "A Compelling Reason for Rigorous Training of the Mind"[1]:

> . . . [A] basic and compelling reason for education—the rigorous training of the mind—is so that a person can read the Bible with understanding. . . . This is an overwhelming argument for giving our children a disciplined and rigorous training in how to think an author's thoughts after him from a text—especially a biblical text. An alphabet must be learned, as well as vocabulary, grammar, syntax, the rudiments of logic, and the way meaning is imparted through sustained connections of sentences and paragraphs.

Of the limitless gifts God has bestowed upon us, one of the most precious is undoubtedly our language. May we never underestimate its power to transmit the good news of God's Word. Remember the reaction of the residents of Jerusalem when Ezra and Nehemiah revived the tradition of reading the Law aloud in the open square:

> And all the people went their way to eat and drink, to send portions and rejoice greatly, because they understood the words that were declared to them. [Nehemiah 8:12]

Let us be faithful servants who appreciate and seek to master our medium: His precious gift of language.

—*Note by Duane Bolin and Amber Densmer*

---

1. Accessed at http://www.desiringGod.org/library/fresh_words/2005/071305.html on August 4, 2005

Section Two
Answer Guide

This page intentionally left blank.

Grammar 5: Sheet 1 Answer Guide

Passage

Henry Reed, p. 30:

Mom or Dad: Please review **nouns**, **verbs**, and **dashes**. We highlight **being verbs** and **homonyms** on today's Activity Sheet. For a review of concepts and examples, please consult the *Grammar Guide* found in the Section 3: Resources. Then read through today's F.Y.I. and have your children answer the questions on the Activity Sheet.

Note: We will present lots of basic and advanced grammar information in the first few weeks of the year. Hopefully, most of this material will be both a review and a refresher. If not, just do what you can. Take your time. You have a whole year in which to "catch up" and move forward beyond what most students in any school will study.

<u>By</u> the <u>time</u> we were <u>kids</u>, my folks—that's <u>your</u> grandparents— had sold three <u>lots</u> <u>here</u> on this side of the <u>road</u>. All the <u>present</u> houses were <u>here</u> except that <u>red</u> brick <u>one</u> which <u>you</u> can <u>see</u> over the evergreens. That belongs <u>to</u> Mr. Apple.

F.Y.I. Synopsis: Being Verbs

- **being verbs** tell what a noun *was, is* or *will be*
- They require three parts:
  1. *a noun*
  2. **a being verb**
  3. <u>one or more words to clarify the noun's state of being.</u>

For example:

Bubba **is** <u>strong</u>.
Lisa **was** <u>laughing</u>.
Zachary **will be** <u>awake soon</u>.

Exercises

1. Circle the being verbs in the second sentence. Then rewrite the sentence so you don't use any form of the verb **be**. *(were; Answers will vary: All the present houses existed except that red brick one which you can see over the evergreens.)*

2. Put check marks above the dashes in the passage above. Why did the author use dashes in this passage?
   - [ ] **To indicate interrupted speech**
   - [ ] **For emphasis**
   - [x] **To set off parenthetical material**
   - [ ] **To indicate a sudden break**

3. In the second sentence, use an **n** to label the nouns and a **v** to label the verbs. *(n: houses, evergreens; v: were, see)* When they are part of a sentence, nouns are often the:
   action word   **person**   :subject: of the sentence.

   Note: The word "can" is a helping verb, which we will discuss on Activity Sheet 4. Also note that in this context, **one** is a numerical pronoun whose antecedent is the noun **houses**.

4. **Homonyms** are words that <u>sound the same</u>, are <u>spelled the same</u>, but do not mean the same thing. Words such as "wave" (in the sea) and "wave" (to greet) are homonyms. Underline as many homonyms in the passage as you can. Then choose 3 homonyms and write another meaning for each one. *(kids—kids (baby goats), lots—lots (many), present—present (gift), can—can (of beans))*

5. **Homophones** are words that <u>sound the same</u>, but do not mean the same thing. Homophones may or may not have the same spelling.[1] Words such as "for" and "four," and "ant" and "aunt," are homophones. Double underline as many homophones in the passage as you can. Then choose 3 homophones and write another meaning for each one. *(by—bye (goodbye) or buy (purchased), time—thyme, your—you're (you are), here—hear (listen), road—rode (to ride), red—read (past tense of read), one—won (to win), which—witch (does magic), you—ewe (sheep), see—sea (ocean), to—two (number))*

---

1. See the *Grammar Guide* in the Resource section for more information.

Grammar 5: Sheet 2 Answer Guide

Passage

Henry Reed, Inc., p. 44:

Mom or Dad: Please review **quotation marks** and **attribution**. We discuss **pronouns**, **proper** and **common nouns**, and **subjects** on today's Activity Sheet. For definitions, examples, and/or additional information about any of these topics, please consult the *Grammar Guide* located in the Section Three: Resources.

"What kind of research are you [pro] going to do—pure or applied?" [pro] she asked.

"What's the difference?" [n] I [pro] asked.

"Well, in pure research [n] you [pro] just sort of try and find out things [n] because you're [pro] curious. In applied research [n] you're [pro] trying to find the [n] answer to some question." [n]

F.Y.I. Synopsis: Pronouns

- **pronouns** take the place of a common or proper noun in a clause or sentence
- must use a common or proper noun (called the **antecedent**) before you use a pronoun
- pronouns must agree with their antecedents in both **person** (1st, 2nd and 3rd) and **number** (singular or plural).

    Correct: *Lolly* [3rd/Sing/Fem] bounced into the room and dropped *her* [3rd/Sing/Fem] books on a chair.

    Incorrect: The *child* [3rd/Sing/Neut] bounced into the room and dropped *their* [3rd/plural] books on a chair.

    (**Note:** See Pronoun Chart on today's Activity Sheet)

Exercises

1. Write **n** above the nouns in the second and third paragraphs. *(difference, research, things, research, answer, question)*

2. A **proper noun** is the name of a *particular* person, place or thing. Proper nouns always begin with a capital letter. Write a proper noun for each of the following common nouns: (***Sample answers:*** **school** *Yale*; **national park** *Yellowstone*; **man** *Dr. White*; **dog** *Rover*; **store** *Sears*; **mountain** *Mt. Everest*)

3. A **common noun** is a general word that refers to a person, place, thing or idea. Write a common noun for each of the following proper nouns: (***Sample answers:*** **Reverend Smith** *pastor, man*; **Chevy** *company*; **Empire State Building** *skyscraper*; **Straight Street** *road*; **San Francisco** *city*; **Officer Jones** *policeman*)

4. Write **pro** above the pronouns. *(you, she, I, you, you, you)*

5. The last paragraph lacks an attribution. How can you tell who is talking?

    ☐ **You can't.**

    ☐ **You simply "know," because the attribution is "understood."**

    ☒ **Since only two people are talking, and the paragraph changed, you can assume it is the speaker other than the one in the immediately preceding paragraph.**

6. Every sentence has a **subject**—which is always a noun or pronoun. Subjects are the "who" or "what" the sentence is about. For example:

    Andy climbed the mountain.
    He launched the paper football.
    The **dog** ate my homework.

An **implied** or **understood subject** is not directly stated in a sentence, but is still "understood" by the reader. We often use understood subjects when we give commands:

    "Look out!" or "Please go clean your room."

Reread the passage and draw an arrow to the subject (either a noun or a pronoun) that each of the following words modify. If you get stuck, think "Who **asked**?": (**asked** *she*; **asked** *I*; **are going** *you*; **try and find** *you*)

Grammar 5: Sheet 3 Answer Guide

Passage

Henry Reed, Inc., p. 119:

Mom or Dad: Please review **sentences**, **clauses**, and **sentence fragments**. We introduce **predicates** on the Activity Sheet. For definitions, examples, and/or additional information about any of these topics, please consult the *Grammar Guide* located in Section Three.

"Where are you going?" I asked.

"Over to call the oil company," she said. "I want to find out how much fuel oil is."

She came back in a few minutes and told me that it was fifteen cents a gallon. That meant that if we had three hundred gallons we had forty-five dollars worth of oil. We weren't millionaires but forty-five dollars is a lot more than nothing.

Exercises

1. What three structural features does a complete sentence include? *(it has a subject [who or what the sentence is about]; it has a predicate [a verb] that tells you about the subject [**Note:** these two together form a clause]; it expresses a complete thought)*

2. All sentences should begin with *(a capital letter)* and end with *(a punctuation mark).*

3. Use an **s** to identify the subject in each of the following sentences. **(Where are you going?** *you;* **...I asked.** *I;* **...call the oil company," she said.** *she;* **I want to find out...** *I;* **She came...and told...** *she;* **...if we had three hundred gallons...** *we;* **Look out!** *you—implied)*

4. Underline the sentence fragment in the passage. *(Over to call the oil company.)*

   What features identify a sentence fragment? *(Possible: they are sentences that do not express a complete thought; they lack subjects, predicates or both; it may be a subordinate clause)*

   Is the sentence fragment in the passage acceptable? *(Y)* Why or why not?

   ☐ **Sentence fragments are just plain wrong.**
   ☐ **It is an author's responsibility to make the people who talk sound as good as possible.**
   ☒ **Dialog does not have to follow normal rules of grammar; it should simply and accurately report what the speaker said.**

5. Draw an X next to the sentence fragments.
   ☒ **Only $19.95!**
   ☐ **I won!**
   ☒ **That I spilled.**
   ☐ **Please hurry.**
   ☒ **Because she slouched.**
   ☐ **Stop!**

6. A **predicate** is anything other than the subject in a clause, and tells you what happened to the subject, what it did, or who it "is." Predicates always contain a verb—in fact, a simple predicate is a verb all by itself. Compound predicates contain two or more simple predicates, and a complete predicate is a simple or compound predicate plus all of their modifiers. Underline the predicates in the clauses below.

   a. Greg sniffed.

   b. Cashew slept the entire time.

   c. He stood up and shouted at the top of his lungs.

   d. Robert's wombats were all the rage.

Grammar 5: Sheet 4 Answer Guide

Passage

Henry Reed, Inc., pp. 145–146:

Mom or Dad: Please review **nouns** and **possessive nouns**. We introduce **helping verbs** on today's Activity Sheet. For definitions, examples, and/or additional information about any of these topics, please consult the *Grammar Guide* located in Section Three.

               hv   n

"Who would want a wasps' nest?"

Midge asked.

             n

"A museum," I replied.

      hv   n

She didn't think much of the idea,

but I asked Mrs. Ainsworth if she

                       n

minded if I took the wasps' nest. She

                                 hv

said certainly not. In fact she would

           n   hv

gladly pay me a dollar if I would take

it away.

Exercises

1. Draw an arrow from the following subjects to the verbs that modify them: *(**Who** *would want*; **Midge** *asked*; **I** *replied*; **She** *did think*; **I** *asked*; **She** *minded*; **I** *took*; **She** *said*; **She** *would pay*; **I** *would take*)*

2. **Helping** (or **auxillary**) **verbs** help form a main verb's mood, tense, or voice, and help to express need, certainty, possibility, and probability. They are often used to ask a question. In the examples below, **auxiliary verbs** are bold; <u>verbs</u> are underlined:

   > **Are** you <u>going</u> to the store?
   > I **might** <u>swim</u> on the team next year.
   > **Do** you <u>think</u> she **would** <u>go</u>?

   Write **hv** over each helping verb in the passage. *(who **would**; **did**[n't] think; **would**...pay; **would** take)*

3. Write **n** above the common nouns and place check marks above the proper nouns. If you find a word that looks like a noun, but is being used as an adjective (for example, the word **gold** in the phrase **gold ring**), it is *not* a noun! *(nest; Midge; museum; idea; Mrs. Ainsworth; nest; dollar)*

4. Write a common noun for each of the following proper nouns: *(**Midge** girl; **Mrs. Ainsworth** lady)*

5. Double underline the plural possessive nouns. *(wasps', wasps')*

6. Underline the sentence fragment. *(A museum)*

Grammar 5: Sheet 5 Answer Guide

Passage

Henry Reed, Inc., pp. 176-177:

Mom or Dad: Please review **predicates** and **syllables**. We introduce **types of paragraphs** on the Activity Sheet. For definitions, examples, and/or additional information about any of these topics, please consult the *Grammar Guide* located in Section Three.

I said, "That culvert's too small an/y/how. It <u>gets blocked eve/ry time it rains, and floods all the lawns on this side of the road</u>."

"I think there has been a com/plaint or two about that. Well, I sup/pose we might just as well put in a larg/er one while we're at it." He <u>looked at me and grinned</u>. "How big a one would you suggest?"

"Big enough for me to crawl through," I replied.

F.Y.I. Synopsis: Types of Paragraphs

- **Expository Paragraphs:** present facts, define terms, give instructions
  - ~ Found in encyclopedia articles or informative essays

- **Descriptive Paragraphs:** present a clear picture of a single person, place, thing or idea
- **Narrative Paragraphs:** tell a story; answer the 5 "W" questions (Who? What? When? Where? Why?)
  - ~ Are often found in newspaper articles
- **Persuasive Paragraphs:** express an opinion and try to convince the audience of its validity

Exercises

1. Overall, what type of paragraph is this?
   Expository **Persuasive** **Descriptive** **Narrative**

2. Write **n** above the nouns in the first paragraph only. *(culvert, time, lawns, side, road)*

3. Underline the complete predicate of the second sentence. *(gets blocked every time it rains, and floods all the lawns on this side of the road)*
   Challenge: What kind of predicate is this?
   A predicate adjective **A predicate noun**
   A simple predicate **A compound predicate**

4. Double underline a compound predicate in the second paragraph. *(looked at me and grinned)*

5. Put slashes between the syllables in the following words: **anyhow, every, complaint, suppose, larger,** and **looked.** *(an/y/how, eve/ry, com/plaint, sup/pose, larg/er, looked)*

6. Identify the verbs that modify these subjects. (**I** <u>*said*</u>; **culvert** <u>*is*</u>; **It** <u>*gets blocked*</u> and <u>*floods*</u>; **it** <u>*rains*</u>; **I** <u>*think*</u>; **complaint** <u>*has been*</u>; **I** <u>*suppose*</u>; **we** <u>*might put*</u>; **we** <u>*are*</u>; **he** <u>*looked*</u> and <u>*grinned*</u>; **you** <u>*would suggest*</u>; **I** <u>*replied*</u>)

   Mom or Dad: The word **there** at the beginning of the second paragraph is an **expletive**—a word that means nothing, but takes the place of a word you would expect to see. They are not the subjects of their sentences. In today's dictation, the real subject is a compound: **a complaint or two.** And the sentence simply declares that such one or two complaints "has been."

Grammar 5: Sheet 6 Answer Guide

Passage

Call it Courage, p. 18:

Mom or Dad: Please review **articles** and **possessive pronouns**. We introduce **types of sentences**, **similes**, and **metaphors** here.

       art   art

The boy stood there <u>taut as a</u>

            ✓pro

<u>drawn arrow awaiting its release.</u>

   art   pro

Off to the south somewhere there

             pro   art

were other islands…. He drew a

         pro   ✓pro

deep breath. If he could win his

    art   pro

way to a distant island, he could

    art   pro

make a place for himself among

        pro

strangers. And he would never

             pro

return to Hikueru until he should

         pro

have proven himself!

F.Y.I. Synopsis: Types of Sentences

- **Declarative sentences** state an idea. These sentences usually end in a period, though sometimes they end in an exclamation point. "My, that reeks." and "I think it's time to take out the trash." are both declarative sentences.

- **Imperative sentences** give advice or instructions, make requests, or express a command. "Here, take this." and "Go long!" are imperative sentences.

- **Interrogative sentences** ask direct questions and end with a question mark. "Will you throw that to me?" and "Are you sure you'll catch it?" are interrogative sentences.

- **Exclamatory sentences** express strong opinions by making an exclamation. "Yikes!" and "Gross!" are both exclamatory sentences.

Exercises

1. In the passage, what type of sentence is the first one?

   Imperative Interrogative Exclamatory ⟦Declarative⟧

2. What type of sentence is the last one?

   Imperative Interrogative ⟦Exclamatory⟧ Declarative

3. Write the verbs from the passage that go with the following subjects: (**boy** *stood*; **islands** *were*; **he** *drew*; **he** *could win*; **he** *could make*; **he** *would return*; **he** *should have proven*)

4. Write **pro** above the pronouns. **Hint: Himself** and **somewhere** are pronouns. *(its, somewhere, He, he, his, he, himself, he, he, himself)*

   Most of the pronouns in today's passage are:

   feminine ⟦masculine⟧ neutral

   Draw check marks above any possessive pronouns. *(its, his)*

5. Write **art** above the articles. *(The, a, the, a, a, a)*

6. Authors often use **similes** and **metaphors** to make descriptions in their writing come alive. Similes and metaphors make comparisons between two things that may not have much in common…except for one important characteristic:

   Similes use the word "like" or "as" to make the connection in the comparison.

   > He was as unpredictable as a worn out jack in the box.
   > She shrieked like a howler monkey.

   Metaphors compare by stating that something IS something else.

   > Rodney was a moving train wreck, dropping books and writing utensils all the way to his desk.
   > His desk was a toxic waste site—I sometimes held my breath when I walked past.

   Underline the simile in the passage. *(taut as a drawn arrow awaiting its release)*

   Now write a metaphor to describe how the boy stood. *(Possible: The boy was a sentry, standing tense, alert, and ready for action.)*

Grammar 5: Sheet 7 Answer Guide

Passage

Call it Courage, p. 58:

Mom or Dad: Please review **italics**. We introduce **adjectives**, **synonyms**, and **antonyms** here.

art
Mafatu had discovered a mul-
art
berry tree. He stripped off the bark
art
and removed the inner white lining.
art
Then he wet the fiber and laid it
art
upon a flat stone and set about beat-
art   art
ing it with a stick of wood. The fiber
art
spread and grew thinner under the
art
persistent beating. Soon he had a
art
yard of "cloth" to serve as a *pareu*. It

was soft and white, and now at last

he was clothed.

F.Y.I.: Adjectives

Is your bed *soft*? Do you have *long* legs? Will you wear *blue* jeans tomorrow? The words *soft, long* and *blue* are all **adjectives**—words that describe or modify nouns. They add to our understanding of nouns. If we told you about Duane's *greasy, slimy, smelly* lunch box, you would have a very different picture in your mind than when we told you about Robert's *shiny, squeaky clean* lunch box.

Exercises

1. Draw arrows from the adjectives in the passage to the nouns they modify. Do not include articles. **(tree** *mulberry*; **lining** *inner white*; **stone** *flat*; **beating** *persistent*)

2. **Synonyms** are two words that have the same (or nearly the same) meaning:

   good—great   *bad—awful*

   Antonyms are two words or ideas that have opposite meanings:

   hard—soft   *sharp—dull*

   Think of two antonyms each for the following words. Feel free to use prepositional phrases, clauses, or other longer means of expressing the opposite idea! **(Sample answers:** **inner**–*outer, outside*; **white**–*black, dark*; **wet**–*dry, parched*; **flat**–*curved, pointed*; **thinner**–*thicker, fuller, bulkier*; **soft**–*hard, rough*)

3. Write the verbs that modify the following subjects: **(Mafatu** *had discovered*; **He** *stripped [and] removed*; **he** *wet, laid, [and] set about*; **fiber** *spread [and] grew*; **he** *had*)

4. Write **art** above the articles. (*a, the, the, the, a, a, The, the, a, a*)

5. Why is **pareu** italicized? (Check one.)
   - ☐ **Because it is a title.**
   - ☐ **For emphasis.**
   - ☒ **Because it is a foreign word.**
   - ☐ **So we can tell that the author is calling attention to it as a word; we ought not to read it as an integral part of the sentence.**

   Mom or Dad: Italicization of a foreign word helps notify the reader that he should not try to pronounce the word as if it were written in English, nor should he think that the author or publisher happened to misspell the word!

Grammar 5: Sheet 8 Answer Guide

Passage

Call it Courage, p. 79:

Mom or Dad: Please review **antecedents** and **syllables**. We introduce **coordinating conjunctions** on today's Activity Sheet.

<pre>
                        pro   pro
Never again need he hang his
  n   pro   n   pro
head before his peo/ple. He had
           n   n   cc   pro
fought the sea for life and won. He
              pro   pro
had sus/tained him/self by his own
  n   cc   n   pro   n
wits and skill. He had faced lone/li/
   cc   n   cc   n
ness and dan/ger and death, if not
                 n
without flinching, at least with
   n   pro
cour/age. He had been, sometimes,
              cc   pro
deep/ly a/fraid, but he had faced
  n   cc   pro   pro
fear and faced it down. Sure/ly that
           n
could be called courage.
</pre>

F.Y.I.: Coordinating Conjunctions

Coordinating conjunctions connect words, phrases or clauses of equal importance. Since there are only seven coordinating conjunctions, remember them by memorizing the acronym **FAN BOYS**:

For	But
And	Or
Nor	Yet
	So

Exercises

1. Write **cc** above all the coordinating conjunctions. *(and [won]; and [skill]; and [danger]; and [death]; but; and [faced])*

   Mom or Dad: In this passage, **for** serves as a preposition in the prepositional phrase **for life**, so we have not marked as a coordinating conjunction. We will discuss prepositional phrases on Sheet 9.

2. Write the verbs that modify the following subjects. (**he** *need hang*; **He** *had fought* [and] *won*; **He** *had sustained*; **He** *had faced*; **He** *had been*; **he** *had faced* [and] *faced*; **that** *could be called*)

3. Write **n** above the nouns. **Hint**: In this dictation, **flinching** is a noun. *(head, people, sea, life, wits, skill, loneliness, danger, death, flinching, courage, fear, courage)*

4. Write **pro** above the pronouns. **Hint**: The word **that** in the final sentence is a pronoun. *(he, his, his, He, He, himself, his, He, He, he, it, that)*

5. Use slashes to divide into syllables: *(peo/ple, sus/tained, him/self, lone/li/ness, dan/ger, cour/age, deep/ly, a/fraid, Sure/ly)*

6. Write two new verbs for the sentence **He had fought the sea for life and won.** (*Sample answers:* He had conquered the sea; He had wrestled with the sea; He had battled the sea...)

7. Circle the antecedent of **it** in the next-to-last sentence. *(fear)*

8. Rewrite the second sentence as if Mafatu was speaking. (*Sample answer:* "I fought the sea for life and won," boasted Mafatu.)

Grammar 5: Sheet 9 Answer Guide

Passage

Red Sand, Blue Sky, p. 18:

Mom or Dad: Please review **hyphens**. We introduce **prepositions, objects of prepositions, prepositional phrases**.

Sand and scrub! She'd never seen

anything (**prep** like **op** this) before (**prep** in her

op life)—a vast expanse (**prep** of **op** desert sand)

just lying (**prep** in **op** wait) (**prep** for a stray willy-

willy) to stir it (**prep** into **op** life)—a sea (**op** of

sun-burnt red **prep** country) dotted (**prep** with

op spinifex and **op** mulga, stunted **op** bushes

and little old wizened **op** trees). (**prep** In the

op distance), the **s** land **v** met the brilliance

(**prep** of the **op** blue sky) (**prep** at a **op** stark horizon).

F.Y.I. Synopsis: Prepositions, Objects of Prepositions, and Prepositional Phrases

- **Prepositions** tell you *where, when,* or *how* something takes place. Most prepositions indicate *direction* or *position.* Ex. **Over** the river; **through** the woods

- The prepositions **of, by, for,** and **with** describe logical relationships between things.

   He danced **with** me all night.
   I brought cookies **for** you.

- Prepositions usually require an object—a noun or pronoun, called the **object of the preposition**—to tell you the *cause* of the action or *where* it takes place, or by whom or what it happens; it completes the meaning of the preposition.

   Kristi hit the ball **over** the <u>net</u>.
   Zach's airplane landed **behind** the <u>couch</u>.

- The **preposition** and the **object of the preposition** put together is called a **prepositional phrase**.

   (**Across** the <u>street</u>), children played.

- Prepositions may have more than one object, which are called **compound objects**.

   When the doorbell rang, Patch scrambled (**over** a <u>sweatshirt</u>, a forgotten math <u>book</u>, a guitar <u>case</u> and finally a bean <u>bag</u>) in order to greet whoever had come to pay him a visit.

Exercises

1. Write **prep** above all prepositions, **op** above all objects of prepositions, and draw parentheses around all prepositional phrases. *(like **this**; in her **life**; of desert **sand**; in **wait**; for a stray **willy-willy**; into **life**; of sun-burnt red **country**; with **spinifex** and **mulga**, stunted **bushes** and little old wizened **trees**; In the **distance**; of the blue **sky**; at a stark **horizon**)*

2. Use at least two prepositional phrases to describe something. You may use two sentences if you like. When you have completed the assignment, circle the prepositional phrases. *(**Mom or Dad:** Solutions will vary; just ensure the descriptions include prepositional phrases! **Sample answers:** My cat, <u>with only three legs</u>, is more agile than my dog. He can drive the dog <u>to distraction.</u> –OR– The old woman <u>with the pearl necklace</u> found herself <u>in a tight spot</u> one night when the lights went out <u>in Santa Monica.</u>)*

3. Is **Sand and scrub!** a complete sentence or a fragment?   **Complete sentence**   **Fragment**
Why?
   - [ ] It communicates a complete thought
   - [ ] It lacks a subject.
   - [x] It lacks a predicate.
   - [ ] It includes both subject and predicate
   - [ ] It is a dependent clause.

4. **Sand and scrub!** ends with an exclamation point which means it is (an):

   Interjection   Interrogative   Exclamatory   Imperative

5. Write **s** above the subject and **v** above the verb of the last sentence. *(**s:** land; **v:** met)*

6. Overall, what type of paragraph is this? *(Descriptive)*

Grammar 5: Sheet 10 Answer Guide

Passage

Red Sand, Blue Sky, p. 23:

Mom or Dad: Today we introduce **linking verbs, predicate adjectives** and **predicate nouns,** and review **helping verbs** on the Activity Sheet.

This moun/tain range was so [**lv**]

dif/fer/ent [**pa**] (from those) [**prep op**] she'd seen [**hv**]

be/fore [**prep**] (in the coun/try) [**op**] north (of [**prep**]

Melbourne). [**op**] This was old and worn;

worn down (by mil/lions) (of years) [**prep op prep op**]

(of wind and rain). [**prep op op**] Amy suddenly

un/der/stood what peo/ple meant

when they said Australia was an old

land and (for a moment) [**prep op**] felt small

and in/sig/ni/fi/cant next (to these [**prep**]

ancient red giants). [**op**]

F.Y.I.: Linking and Helping Verbs

Linking verbs link the subject of the sentence to the predicate noun or adjectives. They describe the way things *are* or *seem* to be.

> The kids *are* sweaty.
> He *seems* happy.

Helping / LinkingVerbs				
am	is	are	was	were
have		do		can
has		does		shall
had		did		will
be		may		should
being		might		would
been		must		could

The linked nouns or adjectives are called **predicate nouns** or **predicate adjectives**.

> Sue *is* a **nurse**. (predicate noun)
> That *seems* **backward**. (predicate adjective)

Helping verbs are always used *with* another verb. They control verb tenses and help to express a sense of necessity, certainty, probability or possibility.

> Victor *might* **go** tomorrow
> Katie *will* **leave** soon.

Exercises

1. Write **lv** above the linking verb in the first sentence. Then write **pa** over the predicate adjective. *(was; different)*

2. Write **hv** above the helping verb in the first sentence. *(had—she'd)*

3. Write **prep** above all prepositions, **op** above all objects of prepositions, and draw parentheses around all prepositional phrases. *(from **those**; in the **country**; of **Melbourne**; by **millions**; of **years**; of **wind** and **rain**; for a **moment**; to these ancient red **giants**)*

4. Put slashes between the syllables of: *(moun/tain, dif/fer/ent, be/fore, coun/try, mil/lions, un/der/stood, peo/ple, in/sig/nif/i/cant)*

5. Draw an arrow from **they** in the last sentence to its antecedent. *(they-people)*

6. Rewrite the last sentence as two shorter sentences. (***Sample answer:*** *Amy suddenly understood what people meant when they said Australia was an old land. For a moment, she felt small and insignificant next to these ancient red giants. –OR– Amy felt small and insignificant next to these ancient red giants. Suddenly she understood what people meant when they said Australia was an old land.)*

If you are a fan of American country music, you may be familiar with the Rodney Atkins song "A Man on a Tractor" (2006)—a song that could be renamed "The Prepositional Phrase Song." If you have time, challenge your children to determine why.

Last line of the chorus:
"...like a man on a tractor with a dog in a field."

Grammar 5: Sheet 11 Answer Guide

Passage

Red Sand, Blue Sky, p. 44:

Mom or Dad: We introduce **voice**—both **active** and **passive**, and **coordinating conjunctions** on today's Activity Sheet.

     s   hv   v   prep art adj

They were standing on a little

 adj   op   cc

rocky beach and in front of her a

sheer rock face rose majestically to

meet the sky. A waterhole had been

eroded out of the red rock at the

        cc

foot of the cliff and lay shadowed

 art

from the late afternoon sun. The

        cc

water looked so inviting—cool and

still, <u>a mirror of dark green</u>.

F.Y.I. Synopsis: Voice

- The term **voice** describes whether the subject of a sentence performs the action of the sentence, or if it is acted upon.
  - ~ An **active-voice** sentence states *who* did the <u>action</u>. e.g., The *waitress* <u>served</u> our dessert.
  - ~ In **passive-voice** sentences, the subject of the sentence is acted upon, but does not perform the action. e.g., The dessert <u>was brought</u>.
- There are two key indicators of passive sentences.
  1. If a sentence doesn't tell you *who* is doing the action, it is written in passive voice.
  2. *-ing* endings on verbs mean the verb serves as a noun (and is called a *gerund*) or an adjective (and is called a *participle*). Gerunds and participles weaken writing and indicate passive voice.
- In order to make passive sentences active, you need to:
  1. provide information about who or what performs the action.

2. make sure the subject is the one that acts.

- A sentence is still passive if the subject of a sentence serves as the object of the verb and does not perform the action.

                     s   hv   v   prep op

Passive: The project <u>was completed</u> by *Simon*.

Active: *Simon* <u>completed</u> the project. 👍

Exercises

1. **Adverbs** modify our understanding of verbs. Often (but not always!), adverbs end in *–ly*. Adverbs can also modify or describe an <u>adjective</u> or another *adverb*.

   Tim arrived in a *ridiculously* <u>hideous</u> sweater. Mike drove *unbelievably safely.*

   Write the adverbs that modify the following verbs or adjectives: **(rose** *<u>majestically</u>;* **eroded** *<u>out</u>;* **afternoon** *<u>late</u>)*

2. Write the adjectives that modify the following nouns: **(beach** *<u>little rocky</u>;* **face** *<u>sheer rock</u>;* **rock** *<u>red</u>;* **sun** *<u>afternoon</u>;* **water** *<u>inviting, cool, still</u>;* **green** *<u>dark</u>)*

3. Analyze the first clause: **They were standing....** Label each word using one of the following abbreviations.
   a. Identify the subject (**s**) and verb (**v**). *(s: They;* **v:** *standing)*
   b. Label the helping verb (**hv**). *(hv: were)*
   c. Write **art** above the article. *(art: a)*
   d. Write **prep** above the preposition and **op** above the object of preposition. *(prep: on;* **op:** *beach)*
   e. Label the adjectives (**adj**). *(adj: little;* **adj:** *rocky)*

4. **A waterhole had been eroded out of the red rock at the foot of the cliff** is written in the passive voice. Please rewrite it in the active voice. *(Sample answer: Falling water had eroded a waterhole out of the red rock at the foot of the cliff.)*

5. Write **cc** above all the coordinating conjunctions. *(and [in front]; and [lay shadowed]; and [still])*

6. Underline the metaphor. *(a mirror of dark green)* Write your own metaphor for something with which you are familiar. Use the metaphor from this passage as a model. *(Sample answer: her face was a hard shell)*

Grammar 5: Sheet 12 Answer Guide

Passage

Red Sand, Blue Sky, p. 53:

Mom or Dad: Please review **semicolons**. Also note the British spelling of **realized/realised**. Feel free to spell as appropriate in your country!

      prep   **op**   **pro**
But now, (for the first time), she

realised that there had been a darker
    adj   **s**   **v**   **prep**   **op**
side—those who came (with guns
cc   **op**   **prep** **adj**   **op**
and hate) (in their hearts); those

who set out to conquer and domi-
    prep   **op**
nate (by whatever means) it took;

those prepared to kill.

Exercises

1. Circle the dash. Why is it there?
   - [X] **To set off a parenthetical or explanatory remark**
   - [ ] **To indicate interrupted speech**
   - [ ] **To emphasize the words that follow**
   - [ ] **It doesn't belong there**

2. Write the adverbs that modify the following verbs or adjectives: **(realized** *now;* **set** *out)*

3. Write **prep** above all prepositions, **op** above all objects of prepositions, and draw parentheses around all prepositional phrases. *(for the first **time**; with **guns** and **hate**; in their **hearts**; by whatever **means**)*

4. Place boxes around the semicolons. What are they there for?
   - [ ] **To help join two independent clauses in one sentence**
   - [ ] **To separate groups that contain commas**
   - [ ] **To serve the kind of function that a period does when commas would do**
   - [X] **To provide more substantial breaks than commas would**
   - [ ] **They shouldn't be there; the author should have used _____ instead**

5. Analyze the clause **those who came with guns and hate in their hearts**. Use the following list of abbreviations to help you.

   a. Identify the subject (**s**) and verb (**v**).
      *(**s:** who; **v:** came)*

   b. Write **cc** above the coordinating conjunction.
      *(**cc:** and)*

   c. You should have already labeled the prepositional phrases, so please simply underline the two that belong to this particular clause. *(with guns and hate; in their hearts)*

   d. Hint: "those" and "their" help to describe either the subject or the subject's "hearts"—both of which are nouns. Should you label these words **adj** or **adv**? *(adj)*

Grammar 5: Sheet 13 Answer Guide

Passage

Red Sand, Blue Sky, p. 131:

Mom or Dad: We introduce **independent** and **subordinate clauses**, **subordinating conjunctions**, and **direct objects** here.

         prep   op

"Careful [with that oxygen line],"

cautioned Barbara.

         s   v   adj do cc

"Right." Jack braced his back and

 v   adj   adj   do

lifted Caroline's limp form.

"Now keep this flashlight steady

prep   op   prep op   prep op

[on the ground] [in front] [of me],

Lana," Jack ordered. "I don't want to

    prep   op

trip [on these rocks]."

F.Y.I.: Clauses, Subordinating Conjunctions

As you already know, a **clause** is a group of related words that include a subject and a predicate. Did you know, however, that there are two main types of clauses? **Independent clauses** contain a *subject* and a predicate, convey a complete thought, and therefore could stand alone as a sentence.

    I <u>ran to the store</u>.
    She <u>made brownies</u>.

Dependent (or **subordinate**) **clauses** also contain both a subject and a predicate, but they do not convey a complete thought, and therefore could not stand alone as a sentence. They "depend" on another clause to form a complete sentence. Subordinate clauses begin with *subordinating conjunctions*.

Although I <u>was tired</u> ☞	*Although* I was tired, I ran to the store.
when she <u>awoke</u> ☞	She made brownies *when* she awoke.

Common **subordinating conjunctions** include: after, although, as if, as long as, as though, because, before, in order that, provided that, since, so that, still, that, though, unless, until, when, where, whereas, and while.

Exercises

1. Label the clauses below as either independent (**ind**) or dependent (**dep**). *(Jack braced his back **ind**; He lifted Caroline **ind**; After we get there **dep**; I don't want to trip **ind**; Since you're standing there **dep**; Because Jake was the fastest around **dep**)*

2. Underline the imperative statements. *(Careful with that oxygen line; Now keep this flashlight steady on the ground in front of me, Lana)*

3. What makes a sentence imperative? *(It commands something be done.)*

4. Put brackets around all of the prepositional phrases. Write **prep** above the prepositions and **op** above the objects of prepositions. *(with that oxygen **line**, on the **ground**, in **front**, of **me**, on these **rocks**)*

5. A **direct object** is a noun that *receives* the action or is *affected* by the action from a subject. In the clause "Kyle crashed his car," *car* is the direct object because it is the noun that crashed. When "Anna scrunched her nose," the direct object is *nose* because it is the noun that Anna scrunched. Underline the direct object in the sentences below. *(**Simon dropped the book.** book; **The cat batted the string.** string; **His hand caught the ball.** ball)*

6. Analyze the sentence **Jack braced....** Use the following list of abbreviations to help you.

   a. Identify the subject (**s**) and verbs (**v**).
   *(**s:** Jack; **v:** braced)*

   b. Write **cc** above the coordinating conjunction.
   *(**cc:** and)*

   c. Use **do** to label the direct objects. Hint: there are two. *(**do:** back; **do:** form)*

   d. Label the adjectives (**adj**) that describe the direct objects. *(**adj:** his, **adj:** Caroline's, **adj:** limp)*

7. Write the subject for the first sentence: *(understood-you)*

Grammar 5: Sheet 14 Answer Guide

Passage

The Big Wave, p. 17:

Mom or Dad: Today, we discuss **subjects** in depth.

           s   lv   pa   s

"And if we are not able?" Kino

v

asked.

     s   hv   lv   pa   s

"We must be able," his father

  v   s   v

replied. "Fear alone makes man

       s   lv   pa   s

weak. If you are afraid, your hands

    v   s   v

tremble, your feet falter, and your

  s   hv   v your   your

brain cannot tell hands and feet

what to do."

F.Y.I.: More About Subjects

All clauses contain a subject and a verb, but can you have more than one subject in a clause? Of course! Let's discuss the three varieties of subjects.

Most subjects we've used thus far have been **simple subjects**, which are simply a noun or pronoun by itself.

    Jeff wrote on the wall.

Compound subjects include two or more simple subjects.

    Jeff and **Duane** wrote on the wall.

A **complete subject** includes both a simple or compound subject, and any words (including adjectives, adverbs or articles) that modify or describe the subject.

    Those boys wrote on the wall.
    The tall, brave, and slightly crazy young man wrote on the wall.

Exercises

1. Identify the boldface subjects below as either **simple**, **compound** or **complete**. (**Kevin** ran. *simple*; **Jorge** and **Ben** dashed across the street. *compound*; **Ainsley, Zach** and **Pete** hurried to the park. *compound*; **Ainsley, Zach** and **stinky Pete** hurried to the park. *complete*; Those **paintings** look ridiculous. *simple*; **Those garish paintings** look ridiculous. *complete*)

2. Write **lv** above the linking verbs in the passage, and... (**lv:** *are*; **lv:** *be*; **lv:** *are*)
   Write **pn** or **pa** above any predicate nouns or predicate adjectives. (**pa:** *able*; **pa:** *able*; **pa:** *afraid*)

3. Write **hv** above the helping verbs.
   (**hv:** *must*; **hv:** *cannot*)
       Mom or Dad: If the passage had spelled **cannot** as "can not," we would analyze these two words as: **hv:** can, **adv:** not. However, as a single word, **cannot** incorporates the negative meaning of the adverb and should simply be classified as a single helping verb.

4. Write **s** above the subjects of the passage, **v** above the action verbs. (**s:** *we*; **s:** *Kino*; **v:** *asked*; **s:** *We*; **s:** *father*; **v:** *replied*; **s:** *Fear*; **v:** *makes*; **s:** *you*; **s:** *hands*; **v:** *tremble*; **s:** *feet*; **v:** *falter*; **s:** *brain*; **v:** *tell*)

5. Write the adjectives that modify the following nouns from the passage. (**father** *his*; **hands** *your*; **feet** *your*; **brain** *your*)

6. Write three new adjectives for each of the following nouns: (***Sample answers:*** **father** *old, wise, kind, gracious, angry*; **hands** *thin, long-fingered, ragged, weathered*; **feet** *bruised, calloused, worn, hard, tough*; **brain** *sharp, swift-moving, clear*; **fear** *paralyzing, overwhelming, powerful*)

7. Add pronouns where you think one or two are missing in the final sentence. (***Possible missing pronouns:*** *tell* ***your*** *hands; and* ***your*** *feet*)

8. Circle the homophones of **wee, knot, bee, week, yew, yore, feat, two**, and **due**. (*we, not, be, weak, you, your, feet, to, do*)

©2010 by Sonlight Curriculum, Ltd. All rights reserved.

Grammar 5: Sheet 15 Answer Guide

Passage

The Big Wave, p. 32:

Mom or Dad: Please discuss **infinitives** and **compound words**. We introduce **appositives** on the Activity Sheet.

>   inf
> To die a little later or a little
>   inf
> sooner does not matter. But to live
>   inf   inf
> bravely, to love life, to see how beau-
>   inf
> tiful the trees are and the moun-
> tains, yes, and even the sea, to enjoy
> work because it produces food for
>   prep   adj   op   s   appos
> life—(in these things) we Japanese
>   lv   art   adj
> are a fortunate people. We love life
>   pn
> because we under/stand that life and
> death are necessary to each other.

F.Y.I.: Appositives

Appositives clarify nouns and appear immediately after them. They are usually set off by one or two commas, and either rename or describe the noun (or pronoun). For example:

> Bubba, *the bravest of them all*, was welcomed as a hero.

From this sentence, we now know two things about Bubba: that he was brave and that he was welcomed as a hero. Appositives can also appear at the beginning of a sentence...

> *A speedy typist*, Bo could code a web page in a New York minute.

Or at the end...

> I stared at Sophie, *the craziest cat I know.*

Or may not have a comma at all:

> We *girls* whispered and giggled until Grandma finally hollered up the stairs.

Exercises

1. Write **appos** above the appositive that comes after the dash in the second sentence. *(Japanese)*

   Did the author punctuate the appositive correctly?
   - [ ] **Yes, she set it off with commas**
   - [ ] **No, she did not set it off with commas**
   - [x] **Yes, she attached it directly to the noun it modifies**
   - [ ] **No, she did not attach it directly to the noun it modifies**

   Mom or Dad: Notice that **Japanese** is a restrictive appositive; it is necessary to the meaning of the sentence. Therefore, it is not surrounded by commas.

2. Use an appositive to combine these two sentences into one.

   > Cherie was an attractive girl.
   > Cherie loved to stand with the wind in her hair and her toes in the sand.

   (Cherie, an attractive girl, loved to stand with the wind in her hair and her toes in the sand.)

3. The author uses many infinitives. Write **inf** above each of the infinitives. *(To die, to live, to love, to see, to enjoy)*

4. Why is **to each other** not an infinitive?
   - [ ] **But it is an infinitive!**
   - [x] **Because it is a prepositional phrase**
   - [ ] **Because it is a partial plural**
   - [ ] **Because it is a clause**

5. Put boxes around any compound words, then use slashes to divide them into their parts. *(under/stand)*

6. Analyze the clause **in these things...fortunate people** using following symbols: **s, lv, pn, prep, op, adj,** and **art**. If you find a prepositional phrase, please surround it with parentheses. **Note:** you should have already marked the appositive (**appos**). *(**prep:** in; **adj:** these; **op:** things; **prep phrase:** (in these things); **s:** we; **appos:** Japanese; **lv:** are; **art:** a; **adj:** fortunate; **pn:** people)*

Grammar 5: Sheet 16 Answer Guide

Passage

Born in the Year of Courage, p. 51:

Mom or Dad: Please discuss **semicolons** and review **predicates**. We introduce **sentence structures** on the Activity Sheet.

                           prep

Later they were bidden back (to
 op
the table), and this time the servers
             prep op
brought bowls (of rice). Manjiro's
 s   **prep op**
eyes filled (with tears). The wise
               adj   **s**
man had been wrong. These people
 lv   **adv**   **pn**   **s**   **lv**
were not barbarians; they were
 pa   **cc**   **s**   **v**   **do**
kind—and they ate rice.

F.Y.I.: Sentence Structures

Independent and dependent clauses build **sentences**—sentences which come in four basic structures.[1]

Simple sentences are an independent clause by itself.
    Pam loved green beans.

Compound sentences are two simple sentences joined together by:

    A *coordinating conjunction*:
        Pam loved green beans *and* she ate them every day.

    A *coordinating conjunction* and a *comma*:
        Pam loved green beans, *but* I couldn't stand the smell of them.

    A *semicolon*:
        Pam loved green beans; Amber brought her a can of them every day.

Complex sentences consist of an [independent] and a (dependent) clause.

    (Although they made her lunch sack heavy), [Pam loved green beans].

---

1. For a refresher on independent and dependent clauses and more about sentence structures, see the *Grammar Guide*.

Compound-complex sentences contain two [independent clauses] and one (dependent clause).

    (As long as I'm not interrupted), [I can finish the book tonight], [but I will need to work on the paper tomorrow].

Exercises

1. Evaluate each sentence in the passage. Then circle the correct structure for each. (**First sentence:** *compound;* **Second sentence:** *simple;* **Third sentence:** *simple;* **Fourth sentence:** *compound*)

2. Circle the semicolon. Why is it there?
   - ☒ **To help join two independent clauses in one sentence**
   - ☐ **To separate groups that contain commas**
   - ☐ **To serve the kind of function that a period does when a comma would do**
   - ☐ **To provide a more substantial break than a comma would**
   - ☐ **It shouldn't be there; the author should have used _____ instead**

3. Write **s** above the simple subject of the second sentence. Underline the complete subject of the second sentence. (*Manjiro's eyes*)

4. Draw a squiggly line under the simple predicate of the second sentence. (*filled*)
   Double underline the complete predicate of the third sentence. (*had been wrong*)

5. Write **prep** above all prepositions, **op** above all objects of prepositions, and draw parentheses around all prepositional phrases. (*to the **table**; of **rice**; with **tears***)

6. The author wrote the first clause of the first sentence in the passive voice. Rewrite that clause in the active voice. (**Sample answer:** *Later, the sailor bid them come back to the table.*)

7. Analyze the last sentence. Use the following symbols: **s, v, lv, pa, pn, adj, adv, cc, do.** (**adj:** *These;* **s:** *people;* **lv:** *were;* **adv:** *not;* **pn:** *barbarians;* **s:** *they;* **lv:** *were;* **pa:** *kind;* **cc:** *and;* **s:** *they;* **v:** *ate;* **do:** *rice*)

Grammar 5: Sheet 17 Answer Guide

Passage

Born in the Year of Courage, p. 89:

Mom or Dad: Please review **clauses** and **subordinate clauses**. We introduce **gerunds** on the Activity Sheet.

[Manjiro nod/ded], [although he knew] [he was right]. [The time in the womb count/ed as the first year]. [All ba/bies turned two with the coming of the new year af/ter their birth]. [He was six/teen].

F.Y.I.: Gerunds

A **gerund** is a noun that has been made from a verb by adding the *-ing* ending. For example:

ski ☞ I love *skiing*.

Note: In general, if you use gerunds when you write, you are using passive voice! Try to avoid gerunds whenever possible: I love *to ski*.

Exercises

1. Rewrite the third sentence to eliminate the gerund **coming**. (***Sample answer:*** *All babies turned two when the New Year came.*)

2. Write **pro** above the final pronoun and draw an arrow to its antecedent. *(He—Manjiro)*

3. Put slashes between the syllables of: *(nod/ded; count/ed, ba/bies, turned, af/ter; six/teen)*

4. Draw brackets around each clause in today's assignment. *([Manjiro nodded] [although he knew] [he was right] [The time in the womb counted as the first year] [All babies turned two with the coming of the new year after their birth] [He was sixteen])*

5. Evaluate each sentence in the passage and circle the correct structure for each:
   First:
   Simple Compound Complex Compound-Complex
   Second:
   Simple Compound Complex Compound-Complex
   Third:
   Simple Compound Complex Compound-Complex
   Fourth:
   Simple Compound Complex Compound-Complex

6. What type of sentence is the last one? **Imperative Interrogative Exclamatory Declarative**

7. Analyze the first sentence. Use the following symbols: **pa, sc, s, v. Hint:** you may find a review of subordinating conjunctions helpful. *(**s:** Manjiro; **v:** nodded; **sc:** although; **s:** he; **v:** knew; **s:** he; **v:** was; **pa:** right)*

8. What is the youngest Manjiro could have been? (Suppose he had been born the day before the Japanese New Year.) *(14! The day after he was born, he would be two years old while the American baby would be one day old. One year after that, he would be three years old, while the American baby would be just one.)*

Grammar 5: Sheet 18 Answer Guide

Passage

Born in the Year of Courage, p. 121:

Mom or Dad: We discuss **person** and **number** in more depth on today's Activity Sheet.

Manjiro nodded. [✓n] "Captain Whit-field told me about your friend who [n] escaped from Japan—then took his [✓n] life. I expect he believed he had dis-honored his family." [n]

"Including his ancestors," Dr. [n] [✓n] Judd said. "And he felt that he had offended the soul of Japan." He [n] [✓n] [s] shrugged. "I didn't understand then, [v] [s] [hv] [adv] [v] [adv] and I don't now. Nor do I under-[cc] [s] [v] [adv] [adv] stand Japan's isolationist attitude." [✓n] [n]

F.Y.I.: Person and Number

Which pronoun should you use if you'd like to talk about yourself? (I). Which pronoun should you use if you'd like to tell your mom that you and your best friend are headed to the park? (We). What if you'd like to point out that the dog is the one responsible for the mess in the living room? (He or she). In English, the pronouns we use are defined by both **person** (first, second and third), and **number** (singular or plural). The first table shows the pronouns we usually use to express each form.

Person:	Number:	
	Singular	Plural
First Person	I	we
Second Person	you	you (plural)
Third Person	he / she / it	they

Note: in English, we do not have a separate pronoun for second person plural. In formal English, we may say "you" or "you all," though conversational English might use "you guys," or in some regions "y'all".

Sometimes verb forms are affected by person and number. Let's look at the verb "to be" in the second table.

(**Note:** See table on today's Activity Sheet)

For these verbs that change, be careful that the subjects in sentences you write "agree" with the verbs. Sentences such as "**I** *are* hungry." and "**Frank** and **Beans** *is* going, too." probably sound funny because they contain agreement errors. If you are careful to keep both pronoun-antecedent pairs and subject-verb pairs aligned to the same person and number, you will avoid many agreement errors.

Exercises

1. Write the person (first, second, third) and number (singular, plural) of the following:
   (**me** *singular, first*; **your** *singular* or *plural, second*; **his** *singular, third*; **I** *singular, first*)

2. Write a pronoun used to express the following person and number. (**first-person, plural:** *we*; **third-person, singular, masculine:** *he*; **second person, singular:** *you*; **third-person, plural:** *they*)

3. Write an antonym for: (*Sample answers:* **life** *death*, **friend** *enemy*, **escaped** *captured*, **offended** *blessed, soothed*, **soul** *body*, **understand** *find confusing*)

4. Underline the sentence fragment.
   (*Including his ancestors*)
   Rewrite it as a complete sentence. (*Sample answer: Not only had he dishonored his family, but he had dishonored his ancestors as well.*)

5. Write **n** above each of the nouns and place check marks above the proper nouns. (*Manjiro, Captain Whitfield, friend, Japan, life, family, ancestors, Dr. Judd, soul, Japan, Japan, attitude*)

6. Analyze the sentences **He shrugged** and **I didn't understand...now**. You will use the following symbols: **adv, cc, do, hv, s, v**. Please consider the contractions as two separate words. (**s:** *He;* **v:** *shrugged;* **s:** *I;* **hv:** *did;* **adv:** *n't [not];* **v:** *understand;* **adv:** *then;* **cc:** *and;* **s:** *I;* **v:** *do;* **adv:** *n't [not];* **adv:** *now*)

Grammar 5: Sheet 19 Answer Guide

Passage

Born in the Year of Courage, p. 146:

Mom or Dad: Please review **ellipsis** and **hyphens**.

"Ye're a thief!" the big man yelled.

"An <u>egg-sucking</u>, <u>lily-livered</u>..."

Like a bullet, the older man's left

fist slammed upward into the Irish-

man's stomach, and as the Irishman

bent over, the older man clipped his

art   adj   s   v   adj

neck (with the side) (of his palm).

do prep art op prep adj op

Exercises

1. Circle the ellipsis.

2. Why did the author use an ellipsis in this passage?
   - ☒ **To show a pause**
   - ☐ **So she didn't have to use a comma**
   - ☒ **To show that words were left out**
   - ☐ **To introduce a series**

3. Match each hyphenated example to the correct explanation of the hyphen's use.

   (d) **to join two or more words in compound numbers**

   (f) **to join single letters to other words**

   (e) **to make compound words**

   (b) **to join numbers in scores, time spans, etc.**

   (a) **to join two or more words that form an adjective before a noun**

   (c) **to prevent confusion**

4. Underline the words that are hyphenated. *(egg-sucking; lily-livered)*

5. Why did the author use hyphens in this passage?
   - ☐ **To divide a word on separate lines**
   - ☒ **To create new adjectives**
   - ☐ **To prevent confusion**
   - ☐ **To form numbers from twenty-one to ninety-nine**

6. Put a squiggly line under the simile. Then write a sentence using a simile of your own here: *(Answers will vary: In this new place, I was uncomfortable, like a giraffe in the Arctic.)*

7. Analyze the clause **the older man clipped...palm**. If you find a prepositional phrase, please surround it with parentheses. You will use the following symbols: **adj, art, do, prep, op, s, v.** (**art:** *the;* **adj:** *older;* **s:** *man;* **v:** *clipped;* **adj:** *his;* **do:** *neck;* **prep:** *with;* **art:** *the;* **op:** *side;* **prep phrase:** *(with the side);* **prep:** *of;* **adj:** *his;* **op:** *palm;* **prep phrase:** *(of his palm))*

Grammar 5: Sheet 20 Answer Guide

Passage

The Cat Who Went to Heaven, p. 16:

Mom or Dad: Please discuss **colons**. **Note:** There are three errors in the first two sentences of today's assignment.

> "Run! run!" he exclaimed. "Buy
>   **prep**
> tea and cakes" and he pressed (into
>   **op**
> the old woman's hands) the last thing
> **prep op**
> (of value) he owned, [the vase that
>   **prep**   **op**   **prep**   **op**
> stood (in the alcove) (of his room)
> and always held a branch or spray
> **prep**   **op**   **cc**   **adv** **sc adj** **s**
> (of flowers)]. But even if his room
> **hv**   **lv**   **pa**   **prep**   **op**   **art**   **s**
> must be bare (after this), the artist
> **hv** **adv**   **v**   **adj**   **s**   **hv**
> did not hesitate: No guest could
> **hv** **v**   **adv**   **prep**   **adj**
> be turned away (without proper
>   **op**
> entertainment).

Exercises

1. What is the meaning of the colon in the last sentence?
   - [ ] **What came before is separate from what comes after.**
   - [ ] **What follows is a quotation.**
   - [ ] **What follows is important.**
   - [ ] **What follows is a subtitle.**
   - [x] **What follows explains or expands upon what came before.**

2. There are three errors in the following segment. Please rewrite it to correct the errors. **"Run! run!" he exclaimed. "Buy tea and cakes" and he pressed into the old woman's hands the last thing of value he owned.** **Hint**: The entire segment may read better if you move the attribution. (***Sample answers:*** *"Run! Run! Buy tea and cakes," he exclaimed. And he pressed into the old woman's hands the last thing of value he owned. –OR– "Run! Run!" he exclaimed. "Buy tea and cakes." He pressed into the old woman's hands the last thing of value he owned.* **Errors:** *1. The lower-case* **r** *in the second* **run** *ought to be capitalized since it is a separate sentence. 2. No closing punctuation at the end of "Buy tea and cakes." In context, the closing punctuation should be a period so that* **and he pressed…** *could begin the next sentence—in which case: 3. the lower-case* **a** *in* **and** *should be capitalized.)*

3. Is **Run!** a complete sentence, or just a fragment?
   [A complete sentence] Just a fragment
   Why? (*The subject is an understood you, the verb is run*)

4. Supposing it is a complete sentence: what type of sentence is the quotation in the first sentence? (Circle all that apply.)
   [Imperative] Interrogative [Exclamatory] Declarative

5. Write **prep** above all prepositions, **op** above all objects of prepositions, and draw parentheses around all prepositional phrases. (*into* the old woman's **hands**; *of* **value**; *in* the **alcove**; *of* his **room**; *of* **flowers**; *after* **this**; *without* proper **entertainment**)

6. **Challenge:** Put square brackets around the appositive and draw an arrow that points to the noun it modifies. (*the vase that stood in the alcove of his room and always held a branch or spray of flowers-[the last] thing [of value he owned])*

7. Analyze the last sentence. You will use the following symbols: **adj, adv, art, cc, hv, lv, pa, prep, op, sc, s, v.** (*cc:* But; *adv:* even; *sc:* if; *adj:* his; *s:* room; *hv:* must; *lv:* be; *pa:* bare; *prep:* after; *op:* this; *art:* the; *s:* artist; *hv:* did; *adv:* not; *v:* hesitate; *adj:* No; *s:* guest; *hv:* could *hv:* be; *v:* turned; *adv:* away; *prep:* without; *adj:* proper; *op:* entertainment)

Grammar 5: Sheet 21 Answer Guide

Passage

The Cat Who Went to Heaven, p. 32:

Mom or Dad: We introduce **roots**, **prefixes** and **suffixes** on today's Activity Sheet.

                    n

"But where is the cat?" thought

     n   prep   op   prep

the artist (to himself), for even (in

    n/op   prep

his vision) he remembered that (in

  op   prep   n/op

none) (of the paintings) he had ever

    prep   n/op   prep   ✓/op

seen (of the death) (of Buddha), was

  n   prep

a cat represented (among the other

   n/op

animals).

   int   art n/s   v   n/do   prep

"Ah, the cat refused homage (to

  ✓/op   s   v   cc sc

Buddha)," he remembered, "and so

prep adj adj   adj   n/op

(by her own independent act), only

   n   n   prep ✓/op

the cat has the doors (of Paradise)

      prep   n/op

closed (in her face)."

F.Y.I.: Roots, Prefixes and Suffixes

All words have a **root**, or a core meaning. For example, you know that the words skis, skiing, ski jumps, and waterskiing all have to do with gliding across a surface with some sort of long planks attached to your feet. We can add parts to root words to change the meaning:

Prefixes appear before the root...

    do   ☞   <u>un</u>do.

Suffixes appear after the root...

    do   ☞   do<u>ing</u>.

Some words have both a prefix and a suffix:

    <u>un</u>believe<u>able</u>   <u>pre</u>school<u>er</u>

Exercises

1. Draw slashes to divide the root from the prefix in each of the following. *(ab/normal; im/possible; dis/advantage; un/plug)*

   Draw slashes to divide the root from the suffix in each of the following. *(paint/ings; brave/ly; watch/ful; soon/er)*

2. Underline two words that have both a prefix and a suffix. Write each part of the words here. *(<u>represent</u>ed, <u>in</u>depend<u>ent</u>)*

3. Write synonyms for the following: *(**Sample answers:** cat <u>feline, kitten, puss</u>; artist <u>creator, painter, artisan</u>; vision <u>dream, illusion, imaginings</u>; death <u>demise, final breath, expiration</u>; homage <u>honor, reverence, worship</u>; independent <u>self-sufficient</u>)*

4. Circle the homophones of **butt**, **wear**, **nun**, and **scene**. *(But, where, none, seen)*

5. Write **n** above each common noun and place a check mark above each of the proper nouns. *(cat, artist, vision, paintings, death, **Buddha**, cat, animals, cat, homage, **Buddha**, act, cat, doors, **Paradise**, face)*

6. Write **prep** above all prepositions, **op** above all objects of prepositions, and draw parentheses around all prepositional phrases. *(to **himself**; in his **vision**; in **none**; of the **paintings**; of the **death**; of **Buddha**; among the other **animals**; to **Buddha**; by her own independent **act**; of **Paradise**; in her **face**)*

7. Analyze the last sentence through the word **act**. You will use the following symbols: **adj, art, cc, do, int, prep, op, sc, s, v**. **Hint**: Ah is an interjection. *(**int:** Ah; **art:** the; **s:** cat; **v:** refused; **do:** homage; **prep:** to; **op:** Buddha; **s:** he; **v:** remembered; **cc:** and; **sc:** so; **prep:** by; **adj:** her; **adj:** own; **adj:** independent; **op:** act)*

8. **Challenge:** Divide the first paragraph into two or more shorter sentences. *(**Sample answer:** "But where is the cat?" the artist wondered. He realized that he had never seen a cat in any of the paintings that showed the death of Buddha. There were other animals, but never cats.)*

Grammar 5: Sheet 22 Answer Guide

Passage

Sadako & The Thousand Paper Cranes, pp. 34–36:

Mom or Dad: Please review **contractions** and **negative statements**. We introduce **homographs** on today's Activity Sheet.

     hv adv s   v   adj adj

"Don't you remember that old

  do   prep   art   op   s

story (about the crane)?" Chizuko

  v

asked. "It's supposed to live for a

              sc

thousand years. If a sick person

folds one thousand paper cranes,

the gods will grant her wish and

make her healthy again." She handed

the crane to Sadako. "Here's your

first one."

Exercises

1. Please copy the contractions from the passage in the spaces below, then write the original words for which they stand. *(Don't–Do not; It's–It is; Here's–Here is)*

2. Rewrite the first sentence so that it no longer contains a contraction ("un-contract" the contraction). *("Do you not remember that old story about the crane?" Chizuko asked.)*

Now, rewrite the first sentence to eliminate the negative adverb. (**Sample solution:** *"Do you remember that old story about the crane?" Chizuko asked.)*

3. **Homographs** are words that are spelled the same but have different meanings. Keep in mind, however, that homographs may or may not sound the same. For example:

   dove—type of bird
   dove—to plunge headfirst into water

   The word **crane** is a homograph. Think of one additional meaning of the word. **crane** <u>bird</u> *(crane <u>machine used in construction; to stretch (one's neck) to see better)</u>*

4. Write **sc** above the subordinating conjunction. *(If)*

5. What sentence structure does the third sentence **If a sick person...** have? For a refresher on sentence structures, see Sheet 16.
   Simple Compound ⦙Complex⦙ Compound-Complex

6. Draw a squiggly underline under the independent clause of the third sentence. Does it have a simple or compound predicate? **Simple** ⦙**Compound**⦙

7. Underline the complete predicate of the next-to-last sentence. *(handed the crane to Sadako.)*

8. The first quoted sentence is what? (Circle all appropriate answers.)
   Imperative ⦙**Interrogative**⦙ **Exclamatory** **Declarative**

9. Analyze the first sentence. You will use the following symbols: **adj, adv, art, do, hv, prep, op, s, v.** If you find a prepositional phrase, please surround it with parentheses. (**hv:** *Do;* **adv:** *n't;* **s:** *you;* **v:** *remember;* **adj:** *that;* **adj:** *old;* **do:** *story;* **prep:** *about;* **art:** *the;* **op:** *crane;* **prep phrase:** *(about the crane);* **s:** *Chizuko;* **v:** *asked)*

Grammar 5: Sheet 23 Answer Guide

Passage

The Kite Fighters, p. 32:

Mom or Dad: We introduce **nouns of direct address** on today's Activity Sheet.

"Well earned, flier," he said, and bowed.

Young-sup bowed in return. He exchanged the kite he had been using (for the reel), and for a brief moment the eyes of the man and the boy met. The look they exchanged spoke of their love of flying; no more words were needed.

(with grammar markings:)
Young-sup bowed in return. He [s]
exchanged [v] the [art] kite [do] he [s] had [hv] been [hv]
using [v] (for [prep] the [art] reel [op]), and for a brief
moment the eyes of the man and the
boy met. The look they exchanged
spoke of their love of flying; no
more words were needed.

F.Y.I.: Nouns of Direct Address

"Did you feed the wombats, *Robert*?"
"*Shirley*, I fed them an hour ago." Robert responded. "You did remember, *Elton*, to clean out the cage?"

In the dialog above, can you tell to whom Robert directed his responses? Yes! Since Robert so carefully named each person as he spoke, we can easily see that he was speaking to more than one person.

A **noun of direct address** does just that—it identifies to whom one is speaking. Always use commas to separate nouns of direct address from the rest of the sentence.

"Have you decided what you'll do with your bonus, *Kurt*?"
"Seriously, *Bo*, the website looks phenomenal!"
"*Lance*, why is everything broken?"

Exercises

1. Why is there a comma before the word **flier** in the first sentence?

   ☐ **Because whenever you write a word of admiration, you should always set it off with commas.**

   ☒ **Because when you write a noun of direct address, you should always set it off with commas.**

   ☐ **Because you should always use commas to set off introductory clauses.**

   ☐ **Because it sounds right.**

2. The author wrote the final clause **no more words were needed** in the passive voice. Rewrite it in the active voice. (***Sample answer:** They needed no more words.*)

3. Two words contain both prefixes and suffixes. They are actually the same word. Underline them. *(exchanged, exchanged)*

4. Circle the semicolon. Circle the correct reason why it is in the sentence.

   ☒ **To help join two independent clauses in one sentence**

   ☐ **To separate groups that contain commas**

   ☐ **To provide a more substantial break than a comma would**

   ☐ **It shouldn't be there; the author should have used _____ instead**

5. Analyze the first half of the third sentence (up to the comma). You will use the following symbols: **art, do, hv, prep, op, s, v.** If you find a prepositional phrase, please surround it with parentheses. (**s:** *He;* **v:** *exchanged;* **art:** *the;* **do:** *kite;* **s:** *he;* **hv:** *had;* **hv:** *been;* **v:** *using;* **prep:** *for;* **art:** *the;* **op:** *reel)*

Grammar 5: Sheet 24 Answer Guide

Passage

God's Adventurer: Hudson Taylor, p. 31 (paraphrased):

Mom or Dad: We introduce **parenthetical expression** on today's Activity Sheet.

                        prep

Tears welled slowly up (in the

      op   prep

older man's eyes) as he looked (at

            op   prep

the strangely radiant expression) (of

        op   prep   op

the open-faced boy) (before him),

             prep   op

and he said (in a voice) deepened

prep   op

(by emotion:)

                 prep   op

"I'd give all the world (for a faith)

prep   op

(like yours.)"

     s   hv   v   do   s   v   nda

"You can have it, you know, sir,"

    v   s   adv   s lv

answered Hudson quietly. "It's

pa   prep op   prep   op   cc

free (to all)—(without money) and

   prep   op

(without price)."

F.Y.I.: Parenthetical Expressions

A **parenthetical expression** is a remark inserted into another thought, but does not directly deal with the topic at hand. Shorter parentheticals are set off by commas, but longer expressions may be set off by dashes or parentheses. For example:

> My dad—*your grandpa*—is a very funny man.
> *Of course*, that will only start to stink if you open it.
> Yesterday, I ran a mile *(even though I prefer to swim)* and finished 100 crunches.

Exercises

1. Circle the one parenthetical expression. *(you know)*

2. Write **nda** above a noun of direct address. *(sir)*

3. Write the adjectives that modify the following nouns: (**eyes** *older man's*; **expression** *strangely radiant*; **boy** *open-faced*)

4. Two adverbs—**slowly** and **up**—modify the verb **welled** in the first sentence. Please rearrange the words in the clause **Tears welled slowly up** in three different ways. Place a check mark by the version you like best. (**Possible answers:** *Slowly, tears welled up; Tears slowly welled up; Tears welled up slowly*)

5. Write **prep** above all prepositions, **op** above all objects of prepositions, and draw parentheses around all prepositional phrases. *(in the older man's **eyes**; at the strangely radiant **expression**; of the open-faced **boy**; before **him**; in a **voice**; by **emotion**; for a **faith**; like **yours**; to **all**; without **money**; without **price**)*

6. Analyze the last paragraph. You will use the following symbols: **adv, cc, do, lv, hv, nda, pa, prep, op, s, v.** (**s:** *You;* **hv:** *can;* **v:** *have;* **do:** *it;* **s:** *you;* **v:** *know;* **nda:** *sir;* **v:** *answered;* **s:** *Hudson;* **adv:** *quietly;* **s:** *It;* **lv:** *'s [is];* **pa:** *free;* **prep:** *to;* **op:** *all;* **prep phrase:** *(to all);* **prep:** *without;* **op:** *money;* **prep phrase:** *(without money);* **cc:** *and;* **prep:** *without;* **op:** *price;* **prep phrase:** *(without price))*

Grammar 5: Sheet 25 Answer Guide

Passage

God's Adventurer: Hudson Taylor, p. 50:

Mom or Dad: We introduce **infinitives** and clarify the difference between **its** and **it's** on today's Activity Sheet. If you are using these passages for dictation, please only dictate the first full paragraph of today's passage.

Hudson had been in his cabin praying for only a short while, when he felt so certain that God was going
$\overset{\text{inf}}{\text{to send}}$ a breeze that he got up from his knees, went on deck, and suggested to the first officer that he let down the corners of the mainsail.

s hv lv art pa
"What would be the good
prep op v art adj s
of that?" asked the first officer
adv
scornfully.

"We have been asking God to send
inf
a wind, and it's coming immediately!" explained Hudson.

F.Y.I.: Infinitives

Infinitives are a *verbal* formed from the word "to" plus the simplest form of a verb. "To run," "to jump," and "to dance" are all infinitives.

Infinitives function as a noun, adjective or adverb within sentences. Since an infinitive is based on a verb it expresses action or state of being the way verbs do. Here are examples of infinitives...

...as a **subject**:

To leave seemed silly since we'd only just arrived.

...as an **adjective**:

Martha knew the best time *to start.*

...as an **adverb**:

We scampered to the tree *to win.*

Note: Be careful not to confuse infinitives with prepositional phrases that begin with the word **to**. In the above example, **to the tree** is a prepositional phrase, and **to win** modifies the verb **scampered**. Just remember that infinitives are always **to** plus a *verb.* Try inserting the words **in order** to test if you've discovered an adverbial infinitive. If the **in order** seems to fit, the infinitive is adverbial.

We scampered to the tree **in order** *to win.* 👍

Exercises

1. Write **inf** above the infinitives. *(to send, to send)*

2. People often confuse the words **it's** and **its**. The word **it's** is the contraction of **it is**. The word **its** is a possessive pronoun. Which of these two words do you find in this passage? Circle it and circle its correct definition: **Contraction** **Possessive**

3. Draw an arrow from the final pronoun to its antecedent. *(it['s]-wind)*

4. Why does this passage have three paragraphs?
   - ☒ **Because, when you're writing dialog, whenever the actor or speaker changes, you should start a new paragraph.**
   - ☐ **There is no good reason; the author made a mistake.**

5. What is the structure of the last quotation?
   Simple **Compound** **Complex** **Compound-Complex**

6. Analyze the second sentence. You will use the following symbols: **adj, adv, art, hv, lv, pa, prep, op, s, v.**
   (**s:** *What;* **hv:** *would;* **lv:** *be;* **art:** *the;* **pa:** *good;* **prep:** *of;* **op:** *that;* **v:** *asked;* **art:** *the;* **adj:** *first;* **s:** *officer;* **adv:** *scornfully)*

Grammar 5: Sheet 26 Answer Guide

Passage

God's Adventurer: Hudson Taylor, p. 72:

Mom or Dad: Please review **independent** and **dependent clauses**. Also, please note the British spelling of **traveled** in the next-to-last clause. In American English, when we add the suffix **-ed** to multi-syllable words whose final syllable includes a short vowel followed by a consonant, we do not double the final consonant. Thus it is **traveled** in the United States, **travelled** in the United Kingdom. Finally, there is one hyphen in this passage, however in this case, there is no good reason for its use.

> *ind* adv adv s hv v art
> [Months ago he had taken the
> do prep op adv *dep*/sc art
> step (of dressing) exactly] [as the
> s v ind
> Chinese did]. [He had called down a
> prep op prep op
> good deal (of criticism) (on himself)
> prep op prep op
> (from fellow-Europeans) (for it)],
> *ind*
> [but he was able to mingle much
> prep op
> more freely (with the Chinese them-
> selves), and had travelled extensively
> prep op *dep*
> (in places)] [where most Europeans
> would have been mobbed].

Exercises

1. Draw brackets around each of the clauses in the first sentence. Mark any independent clauses with **ind** and any dependent clauses with **dep**. *(ind: [Months ago he had taken the step of dressing exactly]; dep: [as the Chinse did])*

   Based on your analysis, what is its sentence structure?

   Simple Compound ⦙Complex⦙ Compound-Complex

2. Draw brackets around each clause in the second sentence. Mark any independent clauses with **ind** and any dependent clauses with **dep**. *(ind: [He had called down a good deal of criticism on himself from fellow-Europeans as a result] [but he was able to mingle much more freely with the Chinese themselves, and had travelled extensively in places]; dep: [where most Europeans would have been mobbed])*

   Based on your analysis, what is its sentence structure?

   Simple Compound Complex ⦙Compound-Complex⦙

3. Write **prep** above all prepositions, **op** above all objects of prepositions, and draw parentheses around all prepositional phrases. *(of dressing; of criticism; on himself; from fellow-Europeans; for it; with the Chinese themselves; in places)*

4. **Dressing** is a gerund. Please rewrite the first sentence to eliminate the gerund. For extra credit, write the sentence without an infinitive! *(Sample answer: Months ago he had begun to dress exactly as the Chinese did. –OR– (No infinitive) For months he had dressed exactly as the Chinese did.)*

   Mom or Dad: With the second suggested answer, you may be wondering why we think the replacement sentence contains a true verb while the original uses a gerund. A key clue: the second answer has the subject actually doing the verb. In the original sentence, the verb is the past perfect tense **had taken**.

5. The author used the passive voice to write the clause **where most Europeans would have been mobbed**. Please rewrite it in the active voice. *(Sample answer: It was a place where the Chinese would have mobbed most Europeans.)*

6. Overall, what type of paragraph is this? ⦙**Expository**⦙ **Persuasive Descriptive Narrative**

7. Analyze the first sentence. You will use the following symbols: **adv, art, do, hv, prep, op, s, sc, v. (adv:** *Months;* **adv:** *ago;* **s:** *he;* **hv:** *had;* **v:** *taken;* **art:** *the;* **do:** *step;* **prep:** *of;* **op:** *dressing;* **adv:** *exactly;* **sc:** *as;* **art:** *the;* **s:** *Chinese;* **v:** *did)*

Grammar 5: Sheet 27 Answer Guide

Passage

God's Adventurer: Hudson Taylor, p. 89:

Mom or Dad: We introduce **verb tenses** on today's Activity Sheet. Please only dictate the first three sentences.

           prep   op

Mr. Nee rose (to his feet). All

         prep   op

eyes were turned (to him) as he said,

prep   op

(with quiet, oriental gravity):

  s   hv   adv   v   art   do   sc

"I have long sought the truth, as

adj   s   v   prep   op   prep

my father did (before me), (with-

    op   obj

out finding it). I travelled far and

            prep   op

near, searching (for the Way), but

          prep   op   prep

never found it. (In the teachings) (of

  op   prep

Confucius), the doctrines (of Bud-

  op   op

dhism and Taoism), I have found no

            prep   op

rest. But I have found rest (in what)

           prep   op

we have heard tonight. (From now

     prep   op

on) I am a believer (in Jesus)."

F.Y.I.: Verb Tenses

A **verb's tense** tells you when an action occurs—in the *past*, *present* or *future*. However, since actions can happen once or over a period of time, there are several types of tenses. (Notice that many forms require helping verbs!)

Use *simple* tenses when the action simply happens.

    Simple past: Zachary jump*ed*.
    Simple present: Zachary jump*s*.
    Simple future: Zachary *will* jump.

Use *continuing* tenses when the action continues to happen over a period of time.

    Continuing past: Zachary *was* jump*ing*.
    Continuing present: Zachary *is* jump*ing*.
    Continuing future: Zachary *will be* jump*ing*.

Use *past perfect* tense when the action ends prior to another past action: Zachary *had* jump*ed*.

Use *present perfect* tense when the action started in the past but continues or is completed in the present:
Zachary *has* jump*ed*.

Use *future perfect* tense to express an action that will begin and be completed by a specific time in the future:
Zachary *will have* jump*ed*.

Exercises

1. What is the tense of the second to last sentence?

   Simple Past   ⟦**Present Perfect**⟧   **Future Perfect**

2. What is the sentence structure of **I travelled far and near...but never found it**?

   ⟦**Simple**⟧ **Compound** **Complex** **Compound-Complex**

3. Write the person (first, second, third) and number (singular, plural) of the final sentence. *(first, singular)*

4. Write synonyms for the following words: *(**Sample answers: quiet** <u>soft, gentle</u>; **sought** <u>looked for, pursued</u>; **father** <u>sire, papa, dad, daddy</u>; **travelled** <u>journeyed, went</u>; **near** <u>close, in the vicinity</u>; **found** <u>discovered, uncovered, acquired</u>)*

5. Write **prep** above all prepositions, **op** above all objects of prepositions, and draw parentheses around all prepositional phrases. *(to his **feet**; to **him**; with quiet, oriental **gravity**; before **me**; without **finding** it; for the **Way**; In the **teachings**; of **Confucius**; of **Buddhism** and **Taoism**; in **what**; From **now** on; in **Jesus**)*

   Mom or Dad: The analysis of the prepositional phrase **without finding it** is tricky. The gerund **finding** is the appropriate object because **it** cannot function as such. **Finding** is actually a **verbal**, and since verbals may take objects, **it** becomes the object of **finding**.

6. Analyze the first sentence of the second paragraph. You will use the following symbols: **adj, adv, art, do, hv, prep, op, obj, s, sc, v.** *(s: I; hv: have; adv: long; v: sought; art: the; do: truth; sc: as; adj: my; s: father; v: did; prep: before; op: me; prep: without; op: finding; obj: it (of the gerund))*

Grammar 5: Sheet 28 Answer Guide

Passage

God's Adventurer: Hudson Taylor, p. 101:

Mom or Dad: We introduce **pronoun case** on today's Activity Sheet. Also, notice the British spelling of **skillful** (written **skilful** in the book). Please feel free to spell it in the English that is appropriate to where you live!

    ind   s   adv   v   *dep* sc

[Hudson never doubted] [that

  s   hv   v   adj   do   *ind*

God would answer his prayer]. [Nor

             dep

did it trouble him] [that he, <u>who had</u>

                       inf

<u>barely enough money to support his</u>

<u>wife and family</u>, would now begin

  inf

to require an income of thousands

               inf

of pounds a year to support the

twenty-four willing, skilful labor-

      dep

ers]. <u>[If he was doing God's work in</u>

      ind

<u>God's way], [God would certainly</u>

<u>send in the money required]</u>!

F.Y.I.: Pronoun Case

Did you know that each personal pronoun has three **cases**? A pronoun's **case** changes form in relation to other words.

1. **Nominative**—when the pronoun is the subject of a sentence.

   I hit the ball.

2. **Possessive**—when the pronoun owns something.

   My ball went over the fence.

3. Use **objective** pronouns when the pronoun is the object of the sentence, so it *receives* or is *affected by* the action from a subject.

Michael soaked *me* with the hose.

This table shows pronouns according to case, person and number of the noun. (Please see Activity Sheet.)

Exercises

1. Write the correct case (nominative, objective, or possessive) beside the following pronouns from the passage: (**his** *possessive*; **it** *nominative*; **him** *objective*; **he** *nominative*; **his** *possessive*; **he** *nominative*)

2. Put a box around the possessive nouns. *(God's, God's)*

3. Write **inf** above the infinitives. *(to support, to require, to support)*

4. Underline the parenthetical expression. *(who had barely enough money to support his wife and family)*

5. Double underline the exclamatory sentence. *(If he was doing God's work in God's way, God would certainly send in the money required!)*

6. Draw brackets around each of the clauses in each sentence. Mark any independent clauses with **ind** and any dependent clauses with **dep**. *(**ind**: [Hudson never doubted]; **dep**: [that God would answer his prayer]; **ind**: [Nor did it trouble him]; **dep**: [that he who had barely enough money to support his wife and family, would now begin to require an income of thousands of pounds a year to support the twenty-four willing, skilful laborers]; **dep**: [If he was doing God's work in God's way]; **ind**: [God would certainly send in the money required])*

Based on your analysis, what is the structure of the…

First sentence?

Simple Compound Complex Compound-Complex

Second sentence?

Simple Compound Complex Compound-Complex

Third sentence?

Simple Compound Complex Compound-Complex

7. Analyze the first sentence. You will use the following symbols: **adj, adv, do, hv, s, sc, v**. *(**s**: Hudson; **adv**: never; **v**: doubted; **sc**: that; **s**: God; **hv**: would; **v**: answer; **adj**: his; **do**: prayer)*

Grammar 5: Sheet 29 Answer Guide

Passage

Li Lun, Lad of Courage, p. 27:

Mom or Dad: Today we introduce **personification** on the Activity Sheet.

   s **v** **adv** **cc**   **v**   **art**

He stood up and shoulder/ed the

  do   **adv**

bundle/s again, happy that he was

toil/ing up the mountain instead of

sail/ing over the sea. (The rock/s

were at peace among themselves;

the wave/s were not.)

F.Y.I.: Personification

The brook skipped along under the trees, giggling and laughing, inviting us to kick off our shoes and come in for a dip.

Wait…can a brook really skip, giggle and laugh? No, but the sentence gives you a clear and interesting description of the brook, doesn't it? This sentence is an example of **personification**, which gives an inanimate object human qualities.

> My eraser squeaked an angry protest as I changed my answer a third time.
> The house popped and sighed as it, too, settled in for the night.

Write your own example of personification on the back of the Activity Sheet. *(Answers will vary.)*

Exercises

1. Put parentheses around the personification in the passage. *(the rocks were at peace among themselves; the waves were not)*

2. Draw slashes between the root words and suffixes of **shouldered, bundles, toiling, sailing, rocks,** and **waves.** *(shoulder/ed; bundle/s; toil/ing; sail/ing; rock/s; wave/s)*

3. Think of two antonyms or contrastive words for each of the following. Feel free to use prepositional phrases, clauses, or other longer means of expressing the opposite or contrastive idea! *(**Sample answers: stood up** <u>sat down, collapsed</u>; **happy** <u>sad, unhappy, miserable</u>; **mountain** <u>valley, flat land</u>; **over** <u>under, beneath, below</u>; **sea** <u>land, air, space</u>; **peace** <u>war, turmoil</u>)*

4. Divide the first sentence into two simple sentences. *(**Sample answer:** He stood up and shouldered the bundles again. He was happy that he was toiling up the mountain instead of sailing over the sea.)*

5. Circle the semicolon. Why is it there?

   - [x] **To help join two independent clauses in one sentence**
   - [ ] **To separate groups that contain commas**
   - [ ] **To serve the kind of function that a period does when a comma would do; to provide a more substantial break than a comma would**
   - [ ] **It shouldn't be there; the author should have used _____ instead**

   Mom or Dad: You may want to discuss the missing predicate adjective in the second clause of the second sentence. (**At peace** is a prepositional phrase, and prepositional phrases normally act as adjectives.) The missing adjective is actually an "understood" phrase. We believe the clause is still complete (it includes both subject and verb), but it is true that if the clause stood by itself, it would create a sentence fragment.

6. Analyze the first clause of the first sentence. You will use the following symbols: **adv, art, cc, do, s, v.** *(**s:** He; **v:** stood; **adv:** up; **cc:** and; **v:** shouldered; **art:** the; **do:** bundles; **adv:** again)*

Grammar 5: Sheet 30 Answer Guide

Passage

Mission to Cathay, pp. 49–50:

Mom or Dad: We will introduce **cleft sentences**, **delayed subjects** and the difference between **phrases** and **clauses** on today's Activity Sheet.

    ind

[There was much talking to be

    ind cc   adv   hv   s

done], [and never had Father Ricci

 v   adv   pa

felt so humble]. All his life, he had

had the gift of tongues, and now he

stood begging in this strange land

where he had so much to do, beg-

ging in a tongue so difficult that he

must only sound ridiculous to those

from whom he had so much to ask.

F.Y.I.: Cleft Sentences & Delayed Subjects

A **cleft sentence** is a complex sentence formed when a declarative sentence is divided into a main and a subordinate clause in order to emphasize part of the sentence. Cleft sentences usually begin with the word *there* or *it*, followed by a form of the verb *to be*.

> *There were* many people who came to see us off.

Can you write the original sentence we used to form our example? *(Many people came to see us off.)*

Since the <u>subject</u> comes after the **verb** in cleft sentences, we consider them "**delayed**" subjects.

> There **were** many <u>people</u> who came to see us off.

Subjects are also delayed in questions.

> Who **is** that <u>guy</u>?

Exercises

1. The first sentence begins with **There was....** This structure tells us what about the sentence? It has

A preposition   A metaphor   A passive voice   **A delayed subject**

2. Draw brackets around each clause in the first sentence. Mark any independent clauses with **ind** and any dependent clauses with **dep**. *(***ind:** *[There was much talking to be done]; ***ind:** *[and never had Father Ricci felt so humble])*

3. What is (or are) the antecedent(s) to all the pronouns **he** in the second sentence? *(Father Ricci)*

4. Do the words **All his life** in the second sentence form a phrase or a clause?   **Phrase**   Clause

   How do you know?
   - [ ] It has both a subject and predicate.
   - [ ] It lacks a subject.
   - [x] It lacks a predicate.

5. The author wrote the first clause in the passive voice. Please rewrite it in the active voice. *(***Sample answers:** *Father Ricci had much talking to do. –OR– Father Ricci needed to do a lot of talking.)*

6. **Challenge:** What is the tense of each of the following clauses?

   Never had Ricci felt so humble.

   Simple past   Continuing past   Past perfect

   He had had the gift of tongues.

   Simple past   Continuing past   Past perfect

   He must sound ridiculous.

   Simple present   Continuing present   Present perfect

7. Analyze the first sentence beginning with the coordinating conjunction. You will use the following symbols: **adv, cc, hv, pa, s, v.** *(***cc:** *and; ***adv:** *never; ***hv:** *had;* **s:** *Father Ricci;* **v:** *felt;* **adv:** *so;* **pa:** *humble)*

So what's the difference between a **clause** and a **phrase**? A clause is a group of related words that includes a subject and a predicate. A phrase is a group of words that is missing a subject, a predicate, or both. Phrases always have two or more words, but are never a complete sentence. Phrases often fulfill the function of a single word—they may be a noun, verb, adjective, etc.

A clause: she went to the store
A phrase: without her purse

Grammar 5: Sheet 31 Answer Guide

Passage

Mission to Cathay, p. 84:

Mom or Dad: Please review **predicates**. We introduce **adjective forms** on today's Activity Sheet.

adv   nda   s   v   s   hv

"Yes, Youngest," he said, "we must

v   do   adv   adj   s

give them back. These foreigners

lv   pn   prep adj   op   cc   s   lv   prep

are here (by my favor), and it is (by

adj   op   sc   s   v   adj   do

my favor) that they have their land.

If I keep their gifts, it may look as if

I have let them stay because of the

gifts they have brought me. And

inf

no man <u>must be able to point his</u>

<u>finger and say</u> that the foreigners

have bought Wang P'an."

F.Y.I.: Adjective Forms (or Comparatives)

In addition to providing a simple description, **adjectives** can tell you more about a noun by comparing it to something else. To do so, an adjective will come in one of three **forms**.

The **positive form** describes a word without comparing it to anything else. The positive form is also considered the **root** of an adjective.

Simon is *silly*.

The **comparative form** compares a word to one other thing. Comparative forms often use the *–er* ending, or include the words *more* or *less*.

Simon is *more silly* than Grant. (or *sillier*)

The **superlative form** compares a word to two or more things. Superlative adjectives often use the ending *–est* or the words *most* or *least*.

Simon is the *silliest* kid in the room.

Exercises

1. Put a box around the superlative adjective. *(Youngest)* Write its root and comparative forms. *(young, younger)*

2. Write **inf** above the infinitive. *(to point)*

3. Write **nda** above the noun of direct address. Circle the commas that set it off. *(Youngest)*

4. Underline the compound predicate in the first clause of the last sentence. *(must be able to point his finger and say)*

5. What are the following pronouns' persons (first, second, third) and numbers (singular, plural)? (**he** *third, singular;* **we** *first, plural;* **me** *first, singular;* **I** *first, singular;* **they** *third, plural;* **it** *third, singular*)

6. What are the tenses of the verbs in the third sentence? Use: simple, continuing, or perfect, and past, present, or future. (**keep** *simple present;* **may look** *simple future;* **have let** *present perfect;* **have brought** *present perfect*)

7. Use the standard symbols (**s, v, do, adv,** etc.) to analyze the first and second sentences.[1] **Hint:** **Yes** is an adverb. (**adv:** *Yes;* **nda:** *Youngest;* **s:** *he;* **v:** *said;* **s:** *we;* **hv:** *must;* **v:** *give;* **do:** *them;* **adv:** *back;* **adj:** *These;* **s:** *foreigners;* **lv:** *are;* **pn:** *here;* **prep:** *by;* **adj:** *my;* **op:** *favor;* **cc:** *and;* **s:** *it;* **lv:** *is;* **prep:** *by;* **adj:** *my;* **op:** *favor;* **sc:** *that;* **s:** *they;* **v:** *have;* **adj:** *their;* **do:** *land*)

8. Is the first sentence a good topic sentence—that is, does it do a good job of summarizing the content of the paragraph?

   ☒ **Yes**
   ☐ **Another would be better**
   ☐ **There really isn't a good topic sentence in the paragraph**

   Why? (Discuss your answer with your mom or dad.)

   Mom or Dad: The first sentence is a great topic sentence. It introduces what the ruler says in the rest of the paragraph but, better yet, it really summarizes what the whole paragraph of dialog is about.

---

1. For a complete list of symbols, please find our List of Standard Symbols in Section Three: Resources.

Grammar 5: Sheet 32 Answer Guide

Passage

Mission to Cathay, p. 103:

Mom or Dad: We introduce **participles**, **participial phrases** and **dangling participles** on today's Activity Sheet.

$$\overset{\text{s}}{\text{Matteo Ricci}}\ \overset{\text{lv}}{\text{was}}\ \overset{\text{pa}}{\boxed{\text{unperturbed.}}}$$

"We cannot have these people thinking that we are swayed by their omens and threats. We must go on, $\overset{\text{nda}}{\text{Michele,}}$ if only $\overset{\text{inf}}{\text{to show}}$ them that our God is above such things."

F.Y.I.: Participles and Participial Phrases

A **participle** is a verbal that usually ends in *–ing* or *–ed* (and sometimes in *–en*, *–d*, *–t*, or *–n*) that functions as an adjective to modify a noun or a pronoun. A **participial phrase** consists of a participle and its modifier(s), object(s), or complement(s). Participial phrases are set off by commas when:

1. they appear at the beginning of a sentence
2. they interrupt a sentence as a nonessential element
3. they appear at the end of a sentence and are separated from the noun they modify.

For example:

Duane, *reclining in his chair*, fought the urge to sleep.
Laughing merrily, we filed back into the building.

To avoid confusion, participles and participial phrases must be placed as close to the nouns and pronouns they modify as possible, and the nouns and pronouns must be clearly stated.

Chewing on a chair leg, KD shrieked at the dog.

In the above example, it would appear that my friend KD has some interesting gnawing habits… As written, **KD** is the noun closest to the participial phrase, so it would appear that she's the one **chewing**, when really, the dog is the one who turned the chair leg into a chew toy. This is an example of a **dangling participle**: the participial phrase has been left "dangling" without a clear antecedent. The above example would be more clear if written as:

KD shrieked at the dog *chewing on a chair leg*.

Exercises

1. Correctly use the participial phrase **gasping for air** in a sentence of your own. (***Sample Answer:*** *Gasping for air, Jacob had to pause before he could finish his story.—OR—Ahab, gasping for air, fought against the waves with determination.*)

2. Rewrite the second sentence and replace the participles **thinking** and **swayed** with action verbs. (*We cannot have these people think that their omens and threats sway us.*)

3. Write **nda** above the noun of direct address. (*Michele*)

4. Put a box around the word that has both a prefix and suffix. (*unperturbed*)

5. Write the person (first, second, third) and number (singular, plural) of the following pronouns: (**we** *first, plural;* **their** *third, plural;* **our** *first, plural*)

6. Evaluate each sentence in the passage. Then circle the correct structure for each:
   First:
   (**Simple**) Compound Complex Compound-Complex
   Second:
   Simple Compound (Complex) Compound-Complex
   Third:
   Simple Compound (Complex) Compound-Complex

7. Use the standard symbols to analyze the first sentence. (**s:** *Matteo Ricci;* **lv:** *was;* **pa:** *unperturbed*)

8. Write **inf** above the infinitive. (*to show*)

Grammar 5: Sheet 33 Answer Guide

Passage

Mission to Cathay, pp. 166–167:

Mom or Dad: We introduce **capitalization** on today's Activity Sheet.

The [Chinese] youth, helpless in the priest's grip, yelled his abuse and accusations; the priest poured out torrents of furious [Italian,] and the boy, [understanding the [Chinese]], yelled at him not to speak so to

prep   art   op

the honored <u>Father</u>. (In the shad-

prep art   op   cc   art   adj

ows) (of the starlight and the small

op   art   adj   adj   s

lamplight), the pale, shocked faces

prep adj   adj   op   v   prep

(of three old [Mandarins]) looked (at

op   prep   op

them) (in horror).

F.Y.I.: Capitalization

We're confident you already know some of the rules of **capitalization**. For example, you already know that sentences need to begin with a capital letter, and that proper nouns—like names—should begin with capitals as well.

Have you ever noticed that not every word in a **title** is capitalized...and yet many of them are? Well, how do you know which ones to capitalize? Here is a brief run-down of the rules:

Do capitalize:

- The first and last word

- ...and every word in between except:

Do NOT capitalize:

- articles: *My Son the Marine*

- short prepositions: "Away in a Manger"

- coordinating conjunctions: *Henry and Risby*

The following table describes a few more instances where words either should or shouldn't be capitalized.

(**Note:** See table on today's Activity Sheet)

Exercises

1. Underline the word **father**. Sometimes this word is a capitalized and sometimes it is not. How do you know when to capitalize it? *(Capitalize it when it is a title or used as a name, otherwise it is not capitalized.)*

2. Put boxes around all the capitalized words that have to do with different cultures or languages. Why are all these words capitalized? *(Chinese, Italian, Chinese, Mandarins; because they are all proper nouns)*

3. Draw brackets around the participial phrase in the first sentence. *(understanding the Chinese)*

4. Draw a squiggly underline the appositive in the same sentence. *(helpless in the priest's grip)*

5. Does the word **Chinese**, in the phrase **understanding the Chinese**, refer to the Chinese language or a Chinese person? *(It is unclear! It could mean either. It is probably the language, but the author should have been more careful.)*

6. Rewrite the first sentence so that it is at least three sentences. *(The Chinese youth, helpless in the priest's grip, yelled his abuse and accusations. The priest poured out torrents of furious Italian. The boy, understanding [the] Chinese, yelled at him not to speak so to the honored Father.)*

7. Analyze the final sentence. You will use the following symbols: **adj, art, cc, prep, op, s, v**. If you find a prepositional phrase, please surround it with parentheses. *(**prep:** In; **art:** the; **op:** shadows; **prep phrase:** (in the shadows); **prep:** of; **art:** the; **op:** starlight; **cc:** and; **art:** the; **adj:** small; **op:** lamplight; **prep phrase:** (of the starlight and the small lamplight); **art:** the; **adj:** pale; **adj:** shocked; **s:** faces; **prep:** of; **adj:** three; **adj:** old; **op:** Mandarins; **prep phrase:** (of three old Mandarins); **v:** looked; **prep:** at; **op:** them; **prep phrase:** (at them); **prep:** in; **op:** horror; **prep phrase:** (in horror))*

Passage

Mission to Cathay, p. 198:

        v   art   s   v   prep op

"Come," the Jesuit said (to him)

adv

softly. "Is it not the law in any family

                        *

that the stronger ones shall care for

the weak? Now, here in the Family of

                             *

the Lord of Heaven, is one weaker

than you. You <u>would not neglect</u>

<u>him?</u>"

     art   s   v   adj   do

The boy shook his head.

              nda

"No, my Father, no," he said.

Exercises

1. Write **nda** above the noun of direct address. *(my Father)*

2. Underline the complete predicate in the fourth sentence. *(would not neglect him)*

3. Put an asterisk above each of the two comparative adjectives. *(stronger, weaker)*
   Write the superlative forms of both adjectives.
   (strongest, weakest)

4. Write two antonyms or, at least, contrastive expressions for each of the following words. Feel free to use prepositional phrases, clauses, or other longer means of expressing the opposite idea! *(**Sample answers:** **come** <u>go, depart, leave</u>; **softly** <u>harshly, loudly, with force</u>; **law** <u>an option, a recommendation, grace</u>; **weak** <u>strong, mighty, capable</u>; **boy** <u>girl, man</u>; **father** <u>mother, son</u>)*

5. What type of sentences end in question marks?
   Imperative [Interrogative] Exclamatory Declarative

6. Overall, what type of paragraph is the first one?
   Expository [Persuasive] Descriptive Narrative

7. Why are the last two paragraphs separate from each other?
   ☐ Because, when you're writing dialog, whenever the actor or speaker changes, you should start a new paragraph.
   ☒ There is no good reason; the author made a mistake.

8. Analyze the first sentence plus the sentence **The boy shook his head**. You will use the following symbols: **adj, art, adv, do, prep, op, s, v.** *(**v:** Come; **art:** the; **s:** Jesuit; **v:** said; **prep:** to; **op:** him; **adv:** softly; **art:** The; **s:** boy; **v:** shook; **adj:** his; **do:** head)*

   Name the subject that modifies the verb **Come**.
   (understood-you)

Grammar 5: Sheet 35 Answer Guide

Passage

Mission to Cathay, p. 222:

Mom or Dad: Please review commas. Today we introduce **transitive verbs** and **indirect objects**.

    s   hv   v io   v   adv   s

"He has told me," went on Wang

          adv   s   v   adv   prep

P'an, "how you cared even (unto

  op   prep adj   adj   op

death) (for this homeless stranger),

just as you cared for him himself,

when he was without his family. I

think the same as the dead man said

in his sickness; that there must be

much good in a religion such as yours,

that teaches men to love and care for

each other without hope of gain."

F.Y.I. Synopsis: Transitive Verbs and Indirect Objects

- **Transitive verbs** require two nouns:

    1. one noun to serve as the subject to do the action

    2. another noun to receive the action or to be acted upon—which is the direct object.

- Transitive verbs transfer action from one noun to another:

         s   v   do
    Jake *held* my **hand.**

- **Indirect objects** receive the action of the transitive verb indirectly.

    ~ they always come before the direct object

    ~ they answer "to whom" or "for whom"the action of the verb is done—and who receives the direct object

    ~ are always a noun or pronoun, but are *not* part of a prepositional phrase[1]

    ~ a sentence must have a direct object in order to have an indirect object

Note: Indirect objects are always a noun or a pronoun that is *not* part of a prepositional phrase. Keep in mind that a sentence must contain a direct object in order to have an indirect object.

Exercises

1. Underline the direct objects in the sentences below and circle the indirect objects. *(Mama read **Zachary** the <u>story</u>.; We gave the **puppy** a <u>bone</u>.; Robert offered **Bo** a <u>ride</u>.; Grandpa sold **Mark** the <u>wheelbarrow</u>.)*

2. Write the person (first, second, third) and number (singular, plural) of the following pronouns: *(**He** <u>third, singular</u>; **me** <u>first, singular</u>; **you** <u>second, singular</u> or <u>plural</u>; **I** <u>first, singular</u>)*

3. Write the correct case (nominative, objective, possessive) beside each pronoun: *(**He** <u>nominative</u>; **me** <u>objective</u>; **you** <u>nominative</u> or <u>objective</u>; **him** <u>objective</u>; **his** <u>possessive</u>; **yours** <u>possessive</u>)*

4. Draw a box around the compound words. *(himself, without, without)*

5. Analyze the first sentence through the word **stranger**. **Hint**: **Me** is an indirect object that answers "to whom or for whom the action is done." Technically, the message that was told is the direct object, so in this case, it is an "understood" direct object. *(**s**: He; **hv**: has; **v**: told; **io**: me; **v**: went; **adv**: on; **s**: Wang P'an; **adv**: how; **s**: you; **v**: cared; **adv**: even; **prep**: unto; **op**: death; **prep**: for; **adj**: this; **adj**: homeless; **op**: stranger)*

    Mom or Dad: The last sentence contains an error: since the final clause is restrictive, it should not be set off by a comma—a topic we will discuss later on. Also, the semicolon appears in error. As the author probably means to expand upon what came before it, a colon or a dash is more appropriate.

---

1. Grammarians can't quite agree whether indirect objects are part of a prepositional phrase. Some say indirect objects are never part of a prepositional phrase while others say there is an indirect object no matter how it is expressed. For our purposes, we'll say they are *not* part of a prepositional phrase.

Grammar 5: Sheet 36 Answer Guide

Passage

Homesick, p. 25:

Mom or Dad: Today we introduce **adjectival** and **adverbial clauses** and **relative pronouns**.

                    hv   art

"Good-bye," I said. "May the

     s   v   do

River God protect you."

  prep art   op   art s   v

(For a moment) the boy stared.

When he spoke, it was as if he were

trying out a new sound. "American

friend," he said slowly.

  dep   *ind*

[When I looked back], [he was still

                             prep

there, looking soberly (toward the for-

  op   *dep* prep op

eign world)] [(to which) I had gone].

F.Y.I.: Adjectival and Adverbial Clauses

Remember, a clause is a group of related words that includes a subject and a predicate. You also know that while both independent and dependent clauses contain both subjects and predicates, only independent clauses convey a complete thought and can stand alone as a complete sentence—dependent clauses do not, and cannot.

Did you know that clauses can serve different functions in a sentence? **Adjectival clauses** (also called adjective or relative clauses) usually begin with a *relative pronoun* and serve as an adjective. **Relative pronouns** connect phrases or clauses to nouns or pronouns. The most common relative pronouns are *who, whoever, which* and *that*. For example:

> The child *who left her shoes on the stairs* should come and retrieve them.

In the sentence above, **who left her shoes on the stairs** is an adjectival clause because it describes the noun **child**.

Adverbial clauses may begin with a *subordinating conjunction* and serve as an adverb.

> I filled the tank with gas *before I went home*.

The clause **before I went home** is an adverbial clause because it describes *when* I filled the tank and begins with the subordinating conjunction **before**.

Exercises

1. **To which I had gone** is an adjectival clause. Draw brackets around the clause and then draw an arrow from the clause to the noun or pronoun it modifies. *(to which I had gone—world)*

2. Draw brackets around each clause in the last sentence. Mark any independent clauses with **ind** and any dependent clauses with **dep**. **(dep:** *[When I looked back]*; **ind:** *[he was still there, looking soberly toward the foreign world]*; **dep:** *[to which I had gone])* Based on your analysis, what is the structure of this sentence?
   Simple Compound ⟨Complex⟩ Compound-Complex

3. The word **looking** in the last sentence is a participle. Rewrite the sentence so that you replace the participle with a true verb. (**Sample answer:** *When I looked back, he was still there. He looked soberly toward the foreign world to which I had gone.*)

4. Write **prep** above all prepositions, **op** above all objects of prepositions, and draw parentheses around all prepositional phrases. *(For a **moment**; toward the foreign **world**; to **which**)*

5. The following words are homographs. Think of at least two meanings for each word. We gave you one of them. (**May** *permission, blessing; name of month;* **spoke** *past tense of speak; part of a wheel;* **back** *adv: the direction behind; noun: part of anatomy;* **still** *adv: yet, continuing; adj: motionless; noun: liquor-making equipment)*

6. Use the standard symbols (**s**, **v**, **do**, **art**, **adj**, etc.) to analyze the second and third sentences. (**hv:** *May;* **art:** *the;* **s:** *River God;* **v:** *protect;* **do:** *you;* **prep:** *For;* **art:** *a;* **op:** *moment;* **art:** *the;* **s:** *boy;* **v:** *stared.)*

Grammar 5: Sheet 37 Answer Guide

Passage

Homesick, p. 61:

Mom or Dad: We introduce **topic sentences** on today's Activity Sheet.

> *ind* adv hv s v art do adv *ind*
>
> [Why did I love the riv/er so]? [It wasn't what you would call beau/ti/ful]. It wasn't *like* any/thing. [It
>
> *ind*
>
> just *was*] [and it had al/ways been].
>
> When you were on the river or even looking at it, you flowed with time.
>
> s v pn prep op
>
> You were part (of for/ever).

F.Y.I.: Topic Sentences

Do you think it is important to know how to write a good **topic sentence**? Of course it is. A topic sentence introduces the subject of a paragraph and tells the reader what the paragraph is going to discuss. Usually, a topic sentence is the first sentence in a paragraph, though not all paragraphs have a topic sentence. Regardless, they should be used in every persuasive paragraph and in all paragraphs of a formal essay.

My mom makes the best macaroni and cheese.
The craziest thing happened in the park on Friday.

Exercises

1. What is the person of the pronoun:

I	first	second	third
it	first	second	third
you	first	second	third

2. Draw brackets around each clause in the first, second and fourth sentences. Mark any independent clauses with **ind** and any dependent clauses with **dep**. *(ind:*

*[Why did I love the river so]; **ind:** [It wasn't what you would call beautiful]; **ind:** [It just was]; **ind:** [and it had always been])*

Based on your analysis, what is the structure of this sentence?

First:
Simple Compound Complex Compound-Complex

Second:
Simple Compound Complex Compound-Complex

Fourth:
Simple Compound Complex Compound-Complex

3. Write six adjectives that might be used to describe a **river** (or different rivers). Remember that you can use participles and prepositional phrases as adjectives! *(**Sample answers:** muddy; clear; glassy; choppy; flowing; smoky; in the woods . . .)*

4. Put slashes between the syllables of **river**, **beautiful**, **always**, and **flowed**. *(riv/er, beau/ti/ful, al/ways, flowed)*

5. Put boxes around any compound words, then use slashes to divide them into their parts. *(any/thing; for/ever)*

6. Analyze the first and last sentences. *(**adv:** Why; **hv:** did; **s:** I; **v:** love; **art:** the; **do:** river; **adv:** so; **s:** You; **v:** were; **pn:** part; **prep:** of; **op:** forever)*

7. Do the words **you flowed with time** in the next-to-last sentence form a phrase or a clause? **Phrase** Clause

8. Is the first sentence a good topic sentence?

   ☒ **Yes**
   ☐ **Another would be better**
   ☐ **There really isn't a good topic sentence in the paragraph**

Why? (Discuss your answer with your mom or dad.)

Mom or Dad: The first sentence is a great topic sentence. Everything else in the paragraph is directly related to the first sentence since it replies to the question that the first sentence asks.

Grammar 5: Sheet 38 Answer Guide

Passage

Homesick, p. 101:

Mom or Dad: We introduce **possessive nouns** and **pronouns** today's Activity Sheet.

My mother put her <u>arms</u> around Mrs. Hu. My father took one of Mr. Hu's <u>hands</u> in both of his. "Old friend," he said. "Old friend." He must have been misty-eyed, for he took off his <u>glasses</u> and wiped them.

Suddenly I found myself blinking back <u>tears</u> and I didn't know why. <u><u>I was counting the <u>days</u> (on the calendar), wasn't I?</u></u> <u><u>Then how could a yellow ginger jar turn everything (inside me) upside down?</u></u>

F.Y.I. Synopsis: Possessive Nouns & Pronouns

• We use **possessive nouns** and **pronouns** to describe what belongs to whom.

• In a sentence, we can show that nouns possess something by adding an apostrophe-s ('s) to singular nouns or an s-apostrophe (s') to the end of plural nouns.

• Here is singular noun that shows possession:

   Greg's calculator.

• Multiple nouns in a series: add 's to the final noun.

   Matt and Pam's children.

• Plural nouns that end in *s*, simply add the apostrophe after the *s*.

   The kids' toys. (more than one kid owned the toys)

• If a noun is singular and ends in an *s* or *z*, you can add either a simple *apostrophe* OR an 's to show possession.

   Chris's computer   OR   Chris' computer

• Pronouns change form to show possession. (See table on the Activity Sheet.)

Exercises

1. Place check marks above the possessive nouns and pronouns. *(My [mother]; her [arms]; My [father]; Mr. Hu's [hands]; his [hands]; his [glasses])*

2. Underline the five plural nouns. *(arms, hands, glasses, tears, days)*

3. Circle the past-tense verbs (including helping verbs). *(put; took; said; must have been; took; wiped; found; did know; was counting; was)*
   Rewrite them as present-tense verbs for third person singular pronouns. *(puts; takes; says; must be; takes; wipes; finds; does know; is counting; is)*

4. Draw an arrow from the pronoun in the third sentence to its antecedent. *(he—father)*

5. A **rhetorical question** is one that is asked without the expectation of an answer because the answer is obvious or simply not required. Double underline any rhetorical questions. *(the last two sentences)*

6. Analyze the sentence that begins **He must have been.** *(s: He; hv: must; hv: have; lv: been; pa: misty-eyed; sc: for; s: he; v: took; prep: off; adj: his; op/do: glasses; cc: and; v: wiped; do: them)*

   Mom or Dad: Did you know that **off** is actually a prepositional adverb? Remember, a prepositional phrase can serve either as an adverb or as an adjective. However, if **off his glasses** is an prepositional phrase, then **took** must stand alone as a transitive verb without a direct object, which does not work.

   On the other hand, if we think of **off** as an prepositional adverb, then **father** (the subject) **took off** (verb) **his glasses** (direct object). It makes sense, doesn't it?

Grammar 5: Sheet 39 Answer Guide

Passage

Water Sky, pp. 18–19:

Mom or Dad: Please review **metaphors** and **appositives** before your children work on today's Activity Sheet.

> art   s/n   s✓   v   adv   lv
> "The whale," Kusiq said quietly, "is
> * adj   adj   pn/n   n
> our hardware store. We use agviQ
> appos ✓   prep   n/op   prep
> [Iñupiat (for bowhead whale)] (for
> n/op   n/op   n/op   n/op   n/op
> houses, sleds, traps, fishlines, bows,
> n/op   n/op
> art, and even brooms)."
>
>   ✓
> "But not anymore," Lincoln said,
>   * ✓   n
> repeating Uncle Jack's favorite line
>   prep   n/op
> as he gestured (to cardboard boxes
>   n/op
> and plastic chairs). "You have other
>   n
> materials. You don't need to kill
>   n
> whales anymore."

Exercises

1. Write **n** above the common nouns and place check marks above the proper nouns. *(n: whale, store, agviQ, whale, houses, sleds, traps, fishlines, bows, art, brooms, line, boxes, chairs, materials, whales; pn: Kusiq, Iñupiat, Lincoln, Uncle Jack)*

2. Put asterisks above the possessives, both pronoun and noun. *(our; Uncle Jack's)*

3. Write **prep** above all prepositions, **op** above all objects of prepositions, and draw parentheses around all prepositional phrases. *(for bowhead **whale**; for **houses, sleds, traps, fishlines, bows, art** and even **brooms**; to cardboard **boxes** and plastic **chairs**)*

   Note: In the second paragraph, **as** serves as a coordinating conjunction that means "when" or "while"—it is not a preposition in this context.

4. The series **houses, sleds, traps, fishlines, bows, art and even brooms** could be punctuated differently than it is. Please add and circle the appropriate optional punctuation. *(a comma after **art**)*

5. Draw arrows that point to the dashes. Why do you think they are there?

   - ☒ **To set off a parenthetical or explanatory remark**
   - ☐ **To indicate interrupted speech**
   - ☐ **To emphasize the words that follow**
   - ☐ **They don't belong there**

6. **Repeating** is a participle. Rewrite the sentence and replace the participle with a verb. *(**Sample answer:** "But not anymore," Lincoln said and repeated Uncle Jack's favorite line …)*

7. Draw brackets around and write **appos** above the appositive. *(Iñupiat for bowhead whale)*

8. Underline the metaphor. *(The whale . . . is our hardware store)*

   Discuss with your mom or dad: why do you think this is—or is not—an apt metaphor?

9. Analyze the first sentence. *(**art:** The; **s:** whale; **s:** Kusiq; **v:** said; **adv:** quietly; **lv:** is; **adj:** our; **adj:** hardware; **pn:** store)*

Grammar 5: Sheet 40 Answer Guide

Passage

Water Sky, pp. 54–55:

Mom or Dad: Please review **subjects** and **sentence fragments** before your children work on today's Activity Sheet. If you use these passages for dictation, use the last paragraph only. Skip the quotation marks since there is no larger context or attribution to indicate it is a quotation or needs to be treated as a quotation.

>   **art s lv pa art adj   s**
> "The air is still," the whaling cap-
> **v s lv pa cc art adj**
> tain said. "That is good. But the sea
> **s lv pa**
> current is strong. It is bringing (in
>   **appos**
> siku), [the pack ice.]"
>
> "Pack ice?"
>
> "The pack ice is permanent ice.
> It drifts (around the pole) all year.
> It comes and goes. (In the spring
> whaling season) it hits the pan ice
> and smashes it (into mountains)
> called pressure ridges."

Exercises

1. Draw brackets around and write **appos** above the appositive. *([siku], the pack ice)*

2. Put parentheses around the prepositional phrases. *(in siku, around the pole, In the spring whaling season, into mountains)*

3. The following words have suffixes. Circle the root word and underline the suffix in each. If the root has been altered, simply circle the altered remnant: **whal-ing, bringing, drifts, comes, goes, hits, smashes, mountains, ridges**. *(whal-ing; bring-ing; drift-s; come-s; go-es; hit-s; smash-es; mountain-s; ridge-s)*

4. Underline the complete subject of the third sentence. *(the sea current)*

5. Double underline the sentence fragment. *(Pack ice?)* Is this acceptable? **Yes** **No** Why or why not? *(because it is part of dialog)*

6. Analyze the first three sentences. (**art:** *The;* **s:** *air;* **lv:** *is;* **pa:** *still;* **art:** *the;* **adj:** *whaling;* **s:** *captain;* **v:** *said;* **s:** *That;* **lv:** *is;* **pa:** *good;* **cc:** *But;* **art:** *the;* **adj:** *sea;* **s:** *current;* **lv:** *is;* **pa:** *strong*)

7. Rewrite the first two sentences of the last paragraph so that they form one sentence. (***Sample answers:*** *The pack ice is permanent ice; it drifts around the pole all year. –OR– The pack ice is permanent and drifts around the pole all year.*)

Grammar 5: Sheet 41 Answer Guide

Passage

Water Sky, p. 112:

Mom or Dad: We introduce **negative statements** on today's Activity Sheet.

> *
> The orange-flagged trail snaked
>
> **prep**   **op**   **prep**
> [around huge ice blocks], [across
>
> **op**   **prep**   **op**   **prep**
> open flats] and [along the edge] [of
>
> **op**   **prep**
> the shore] to finally arrive [at a radio
>
> **op**
> tower]. Vincent signaled, "Stop."
>
> **prep**   **op**
> "End [of the United States], Point
>
> **prep**
> Barrow," said Weir, walking [up to
>
> **op**   **art**   ***/adj**   **s**
> Lincoln]. The wind-packed snow
>
> **v**   **art**   **do**   **sc**
> smoothed the landscape so that
>
> **s**   **hv neg/adv v**   **adv**   **art**   **s**
> <u>Lincoln could not tell</u> where the U.S.
>
> **v**   **cc**   **art**   **s**   **v**
> ended and the ocean began.

F.Y.I.: Negative Statements

Negative statements express something that is not true, and usually feature words such as *no*, *not*, *nothing* and *no one*. For example:

> There is *nothing* left on the plate.
> There are *no* more ornaments to put on the tree.

Keep in mind that *no* and *not* can also be adjectives that modify nouns, adjectives, verbs, or other adverbs.

> I can *not* climb the stairs. (adverb)
> He is *not* a dog. (adjective)

Exercises

1. Underline the negative clause in today's passage. *(Lincoln could not tell)*

2. Put an asterisk above the hyphens.

3. Why did the author use hyphens in this passage?
    - ☐ **To divide a word on separate lines**
    - ☒ **To create new adjectives**
    - ☐ **To prevent confusion**
    - ☐ **To separate numbers**

4. Why are some adjectives connected with hyphens and some are not? *(Some are connected with hyphens in order to join two words that form a single adjective. The other adjectives can stand alone.)*

5. Put brackets around all of the prepositional phrases. Write **prep** over the prepositions and **op** over objects of prepositions. *(around huge ice **blocks**, across open **flats**, along the **edge**, of the **shore**, at a radio **tower**, of the **United States**, up to **Lincoln**)*

6. In this passage **ocean** is not capitalized, but sometimes it is. How do you know when to capitalize this word? *(Capitalize it when talking about a specific ocean, and not when talking about oceans in general.)*

7. Use the standard symbols to analyze the final sentence. *(art: The; adj: wind-packed; s: snow; v: smoothed; art: the; do: landscape; sc: so that; s: Lincoln; hv: could: neg/adv: not; v: tell; adv: where; art: the; s: U.S.; v: ended; cc: and; art: the; s: ocean; v: began)*

8. Rewrite the first sentence with a different verb. *(Answers will vary: The orange-flagged trail wound around huge ice blocks, across open flats and along the edge of the shore to finally stop at a radio tower.)*

Grammar 5: Sheet 42 Answer Guide

Passage

Water Sky, p. 169:

Mom or Dad: Please review **sentence structures** and **subjects**. We introduce **nonrestrictive** and **restrictive phrases** and **clauses** on today's Activity Sheet.

Musk Ox held the harpoon where Little Owl had aimed it. [Then suddenly he turned, pulled Kusiq to his feet and gave the harpoon to him.]

        s   v   do   adv   cc   prep

[Kusiq took it eagerly, and, (with

art adj   op   v   do   art   s

a loud grunt); threw it.] [The har-

     v   art   do   cc   v

poon hit the mark and disappeared.]

art   s   v

[The whale plunged.]

F.Y.I.: Nonrestrictive & Restrictive Phrases and Clauses

A while back, we discussed how adjectival and adverbial clauses can add description to a sentence. Did you know, however, that these clauses can be either *nonrestrictive* or *restrictive*?

A **nonrestrictive phrase** or **clause** adds information to a sentence that may be interesting but is not essential to the meaning of the sentence. To determine whether a phrase or clause is nonrestrictive, remove it from the sentence. If the meaning does not change, the phrase or clause is nonrestrictive.

> I winced, *wishing I had thought to move the vase before I'd left those two alone in the living room.*

A **restrictive phrase** or **clause** adds information to a sentence that is essential to its meaning. Yet unlike their counterparts, do not set off restrictive phrases and clauses from the rest of the sentence with any kind of punctuation (commas, dashes, etc.).

> If you eat food *that can stain the carpet*, please stay in the kitchen.

Notice how the meaning of the sentence changes if we remove the restrictive clause:

> If you eat food, please stay in the kitchen.

Remember, adjectival clauses usually begin with a **relative pronoun**, such as *who, whoever, which* or *that*. Adverbial clauses often begin with a **subordinating conjunction**.

Exercises

1. The following instructions have to do with the first sentence in the second paragraph.

   a. We believe the author mis-punctuated the sentence. It seems as though the sentence includes a nonrestrictive phrase, but the author failed to set it off with commas. Please add commas where they belong, and circle the commas you add. *(Kusiq took it eagerly, and, with a loud grunt, threw it.)*

   b. If the nonrestrictive clause is set off appropriately, it should be clear that the original comma is wholly unnecessary. Put an arrow over the comma you no longer need. *(Kusiq took it eagerly, and, with a loud grunt, threw it.)*

2. Do the words **The whale plunged** form a phrase or a clause?   **Phrase**   Clause

3. Draw brackets around the simple sentences. *(all sentences except the first)*

4. **Challenge:** What is true about the second sentence? (Check all that apply.)
   - [x] **It is a simple sentence**
   - [ ] **It is a compound sentence**
   - [ ] **It has a compound subject**
   - [x] **It has a simple subject**
   - [x] **It has a compound predicate**
   - [ ] **It has a simple predicate**

5. What kind of sentence is the last one?   **Imperative**   **Interrogative**   **Exclamatory**   Declarative

6. Analyze the second paragraph. (**s:** *Kusiq;* **v:** *took;* **do:** *it;* **adv:** *eagerly;* **cc:** *and;* **prep:** *with;* **art:** *a;* **adj:** *loud;* **op:** *grunt;* **v:** *threw;* **do:** *it;* **art:** *The;* **s:** *harpoon;* **v:** *hit;* **art:** *the;* **do:** *mark;* **cc:** *and;* **v:** *disappeared;* **art:** *The;* **s:** *whale;* **v:** *plunged)*

Grammar 5: Sheet 43 Answer Guide

Passage

The Incredible Journey, p. 19:

Mom or Dad: Please review **voice**, and **coordinating** and **subordinating conjunctions**.

Twen/ty min/utes passed by and **[cc]**

no move was made; then sud/den/

ly the young dog rose, stretched

him/self, and stood looking intently **[cc]**

down the drive. Then slowly the

Labrador walked down the

drive/way and stood at the curve, **[cc]**

looking back as though inviting the **[sc]**

oth/ers to come. The old dog rose **[art][adj][s][v]**

too, now, some/what stiffly, and **[adv][adv][adv][adv][cc]**

followed. Together they turned the **[v][adv][s][v][art]**

corner, (out of sight). **[do][prep][op]**

Exercises

1. Put boxes around any compound words, then use slashes to divide them into their parts. *(him/self; drive/way; some/what)*

2. Use slashes to divide **twenty**, **minutes**, **suddenly**, **stretched**, and **others** into syllables. *(twen/ty, min/utes, sud/den/ly, stretched, oth/ers)*

3. **Looking**, and **inviting** are participles. Rewrite the second sentence and replace the participles with true action verbs. (**Sample answer:** *Then slowly the Labrador walked down the driveway and stood at the curve. He looked back and invited the others to come.*)

4. The author wrote the first clause in the passive voice. Please rewrite it in the active voice. (**Sample answers:** *For twenty minutes, none of the animals moved. –OR– Twenty minutes passed and none of the animals made a move.*)

5. Write the person (first, second, third) and number (singular, plural) of the pronoun in the final sentence. *(they—third, plural)*

6. Write **cc** above any coordinating conjunctions and **sc** above any subordinating conjunctions. (**cc:** *and [no move], and [stood looking], and [stood at];* **sc:** *as though;* **cc:** *and [followed])*

7. Analyze the last two sentences. (**art:** *The;* **adj:** *old;* **s:** *dog;* **v:** *rose;* **adv:** *too;* **adv:** *now;* **adv:** *somewhat;* **adv:** *stiffly;* **cc:** *and;* **v:** *followed;* **adv:** *Together;* **s:** *they;* **v:** *turned;* **art:** *the;* **do:** *corner;* **prep:** *out of;* **op:** *sight)*

Grammar 5: Sheet 44 Answer Guide

Passage

The Incredible Journey, pp. 25–26:

Mom or Dad: You may skip the last sentence for today's dictation. Please review **participles** and **participial phrases**.

The young dog slept (in fitful, uneasy starts), his muscles twitching, constantly lifting his head and growling softly. Once he sprang to his feet with a full-throated roar which brought a sudden splash in the distance, then silence—and who knows what else unknown, unseen or unheard passed through his mind

adj   adj

to disturb him further? Only one

s   lv   pa   cc   pa   sc   prep

thing was clear and certain—that at

adj   op   s   hv   part/pa   do

all costs he was going home, home

to his own beloved master.

Exercises

1. Underline the five words that have prefixes and circle the prefixes. *(uneasy, unknown, unseen, unheard, beloved)*

2. Draw a box around the complete subject of the first sentence and write **s** above the simple subject. *(The young **dog**)*

3. **Twitching**, **lifting** and **growling** are participles. Rewrite the first sentence and replace the participles

with action verbs. (***Sample answer:*** *The young dog slept in fitful uneasy starts. His muscles twitched, and he constantly lifted his head and growled softly.*)

4. Draw a squiggly line under the participial phrase in the first sentence.
   (constantly lifting his head and growling softly)
   Discuss with Mom or Dad: Do you think this is a dangling participle? Why or why not? *(Yes: The closest noun is **muscles**, but it doesn't make much sense that the dog's muscles **growled softly**. It makes more sense that the phrase modifies his **uneasy starts**, or even the **young dog**. The author could restructure the sentence slightly to remove this ambiguity.)*

5. Analyze the last sentence through **going home**. (**adj:** *only;* **adj:** *one;* **s:** *thing;* **lv:** *was;* **pa:** *clear;* **cc:** *and;* **pa:** *certain;* **sc:** *that;* **prep:** *at;* **adj:** *all;* **op:** *costs;* **s:** *he;* **hv:** *was;* **part/pa:** *going;* **do:** *home.*)

6. Think of two antonyms or, at least, contrastive expressions for each of the following words. Feel free to use prepositional phrases, clauses, or other longer means of expressing the opposite idea! (***Sample answers:*** **young** *old, ancient, mature;* **dog** *cat, puppy;* **uneasy** *relaxed, resting;* **constantly** *never, occasionally, rarely;* **softly** *harshly, roughly, loudly;* **sudden** *gradual, expected;* **silence** *noise, a deafening roar;* **master** *servant, slave*)

7. Why is there a comma between **fitful** and **uneasy** in the first sentence?
   - ☐ Because you should always set off an introductory adverbial clause with a comma.
   - ☐ Because you should always set off a non-restrictive appositive phrase with commas.
   - ☐ Because you should always set off an introductory participial or prepositional phrase with a comma.
   - ☒ **Because you should always use a comma to separate adjectives that equally modify the same noun.**
   - ☐ There is no good reason for the commas.

8. Double underline the rhetorical question. *(and who knows what else unknown, unseen or unheard passed through his mind to disturb him further?)*

Grammar 5: Sheet 45 Answer Guide

Passage

The Incredible Journey, p. 101:

Mom or Dad: We introduce **expletives** on today's Activity Sheet.

It would have been impossible to
comp adv
find three more contented animals
that night. They lay curled closely
prep   **op**   **prep**
together (in a hollow) filled (with
op   **prep**
sweet-scented needles), (under an
op   **prep**
aged, spreading balsam tree), (near
op   **prep**   **op**
the banks) (of the stream). The old
dog had his beloved cat, warm and
prep   **op**
purring (between his paws) again,
prep   **op**
and he snored (in deep content-
appos
ment). The young dog, [their gently worried leader], <u>had found his</u>
<u>charge again.</u>

F.Y.I.: Expletives

In English, an **expletive** is a word or phrase that adds information to a sentence but exists only to help the sentence maintain its structure. An expletive acts as the subject or object of a verb, but needs a following word or phrase to provide the meaningful content. Often, expletives appear as the word *it* or *there* in the beginning of a sentence, followed by a form of the verb **to be**.

> *It was* a dark and stormy night when I first heard the sound.

> *There might have been* more if I hadn't dropped the plate on my way inside.

Expletives add nothing to a sentence. Since expletives act as fillers and can give your message a stuffy tone, seek to remove them from your writing.

Exercises

1. The word **it** in the first sentence is an **expletive**: it means nothing, but it takes up the space where we would expect to find a subject. This sentence has a **delayed subject**. The true subject of this sentence is the infinitive **to find**. Please rewrite the sentence so that its subject comes at the beginning. *(Sample answer: To find three more contented animals that night would have been impossible)*

   Mom or Dad: Infinitives can serve as nouns, adjectives, and adverbs. In this case, the infinitive serves as a noun.

2. Write **prep** above all prepositions, **op** above all objects of prepositions, and draw parentheses around all prepositional phrases. *(in a **hollow**; with sweet-scented **needles**; under an aged, spreading balsam **tree**; near the **banks**; of the **stream**; between his **paws**; in deep **contentment**)*

3. Find, draw brackets around, and write **appos** above the appositive. *(their gently worried leader)*

4. Underline the complete predicate of the final sentence. *(had found his charge again)*

5. Find a comparative adverb and write **comp adv** above it, then write its superlative form here: *(more; most)*

6. Is the first sentence a good topic sentence?
   - [X] **Yes**
   - [ ] **Another would be better**
   - [ ] **There really isn't a good topic sentence in the paragraph**

   Why? (Discuss your answer with your mom or dad.)

   Mom or Dad: It's perfect! How might you better summarize the subject matter of such a brief paragraph?

Grammar 5: Sheet 46 Answer Guide

Passage

Rascal, p. 26:

Mom or Dad: We introduce **subject-verb agreement** on today's Activity Sheet.

    s lv   pa   appos   s

"It is hungry, the little one," she

  v

said, petting the small raccoon. "Go

                                    nda

fetch a clean wheat straw, Oscar."

    s   v   ✓adj adj   do   prep

She filled her own mouth (with

adj op   v   art   adj   do

warm milk), put the wheat straw

   prep   ✓adj op   cc   v   art

(between her lips), and slanted the

  do   adv   prep art   op   prep art

straw down (to the mouth) (of the

  adj   op

little raccoon). <u>I watched, fascinated,</u>

 sc ✓

<u>as my new pet took the straw</u>

<u>eagerly and began to nurse.</u>

F.Y.I.: Subject-Verb Agreement

You already know that nouns (or subjects) can either be singular or plural, but did you know that verbs can be too?

      The boys eats quickly.

We're confident you know the above sentence contains an error, but what is wrong, specifically? Well, the subject **boys** is a plural subject, but it's been paired with the singular form of the verb "to eat". To eliminate this **subject-verb agreement** error, the verb and the subject must agree in both *person* and *number*.

      The *boy eats* quickly. (Singular subject and verb.)
      The *boys eat* quickly. (Plural subject and verb.)

In two special cases,[1] it can be tricky to determine subject-verb agreement:

1. **Collective nouns take singular verbs** because you're

talking about only "one" group:

    Yes: My family *loves* to read. (One family = singular)
    No: My family *love* to read.

2. **Proper names that include a plural noun also take singular verbs** because the whole proper noun refers to one item.

    Yes: I have heard that <u>Holes</u> *is* a great movie.
      (One movie = singular)
    No: I have heard that <u>Holes</u> *are* a great movie.

Exercises

1. Rewrite the following to eliminate the agreement errors. *(child sleeps/children sleep; cats jump...hang/cat jumps...hangs; class quiets...waits; Jacob...runs)*

2. What is the tense of the linking verb in the first sentence?   **Past**   ⸛**Present**⸛   **Future**
What is the tense of the active verb in the first sentence?   ⸛**Past**⸛   **Present**   **Future**

3. Write **nda** above the noun of direct address. *(Oscar)* What are you supposed to do when you write a noun of direct address? (Circle all that apply.)
Capitalize it ⸛ **Use commas to set it off** ⸛ **Make sure it comes at the beginning or end of the sentence**

4. Underline the complex sentence and write **sc** above the subordinating conjunction. *(I watched, fascinated, **as** my new pet took the straw eagerly and began to nurse)*

5. Put a check mark above the possessive pronouns. *(her [own mouth], her [lips], my [new pet])*

6. Analyze the first sentence of both paragraphs. Skip the phrase **petting the small raccoon**. *(**s:** It; **lv:** is; **pa:** hungry; **appos:** the little one; **s:** she; **v:** said; **s:** She; **v:** filled; **adj:** her; **adj:** own; **do:** mouth; **prep:** with; **adj:** warm; **op:** milk; **v:** put; **art:** the; **adj:** wheat; **do:** straw; **prep:** between; **adj:** her; **op:** lips; **cc:** and; **v:** slanted; **art:** the; **do:** straw; **adv:** down; **prep:** to; **art:** the; **op:** mouth; **prep:** of; **art:** the; **adj:** little; **op:** raccoon)*

7. Should there be a paragraph break after "small raccoon" in the first paragraph?   **Yes**   ⸛**No**⸛
Why or why not? *(because the speaker does not change; if the paragraph changed, you would think someone else was talking)*

---

1. See this week's Activity Sheet for specifics on other special cases.

Grammar 5: Sheet 47 Answer Guide

Passage

Rascal, p. 33:

Mom or Dad: We introduce **indirect quotations** on today's Activity Sheet.

Rascal felt the lump of sugar,

sniffed it, and then began his usual

part
washing ceremony, swishing it back

and forth through his bowl of milk.

prep art adj   op   prep   op   s
(In a few moments), (of course), it

v   adv   adv   cc art adv
melted entirely away, and a more

part/adj   adj   do   s   hv   adv
surprised little 'coon you have never

v   prep adj   op
seen (in your life). He looked at me

and trilled a shrill question: <u>who</u>

<u>had stolen his sugar lump?</u>

F.Y.I.: Indirect Quotations

Sometimes, somebody may tell you what someone else said, but not relay the message word-for-word. Usually, this kind of communication is fine, as long as the message doesn't change (and you know, for example, that Mom said to come for dinner *now* rather than "when you feel like it")! In literature, if an author modifies a quotation in any way, the quotation is then called an **indirect quotation**. This type of quotation is not set apart by quotation marks. Consider the following:

> Bubba hollered up the stairs, "We need to purchase another mouse trap, honey!"

And the author wrote:

> Bubba hollered up the stairs that we needed to purchase another mouse trap.

Even though the author's version simply changed the tense of verb *need* to *needed* and omitted the noun of direct address in Bubba's message, the quotation is no longer a direct quote.

The same would be true if we simply modified a pronoun.

> "I need to pick up a new mouse trap!"
> We need to pick up a new mouse trap.

Exercises

1. Underline the indirect quote. *(who had stolen his sugar lump?)*

2. What is the structure of the first sentence?
   (Simple) Compound Complex Compound-Complex

   Mom or Dad: Notice that though the sentence has three simple predicates, it has only one subject. Put another way, it has a compound predicate, but it is still a simple sentence.

   What is the structure of the second sentence?

   Simple (Compound) Complex Compound-Complex

   What is the structure of the last sentence?

   Simple (Compound) Complex Compound-Complex

3. Overall, what is the tense of this paragraph?
   (Past)   Present   Future

4. Write **part** above the participles **washing** and **surprised**. Draw arrows to the nouns or pronouns they modify. *(washing-ceremony; surprised-'coon)*

5. Double underline the parenthetical expression. *(of course)*

6. Analyze the second sentence. **Hint:** 'coon is a direct object. **(prep:** *In;* **art:** *a;* **adj:** *few;* **op:** *moments;* **prep:** *of;* **op:** *course;* **s:** *it;* **v:** *melted;* **adv:** *entirely;* **adv:** *away;* **cc:** *and;* **art:** *a;* **adv:** *more;* **adj:** *surprised;* **adj:** *little;* **do:** *'coon;* **s:** *you;* **hv:** *have;* **adv:** *never;* **v:** *seen;* **prep:** *in;* **adj:** *your;* **op:** *life)*

   For what verb is **'coon** a direct object?

   melted   surprised   (seen)

   Mom or Dad: The word **surprised** is a participle—a verbal adjective; it is not a verb. To help your child "see" the correct answer, perhaps you can turn the clause around: **...And you have never seen a more surprised 'coon in your life.**

Grammar 5: Sheet 48 Answer Guide

Passage

Rascal, p. 118:

Mom or Dad: Please review **independent** and **dependent clauses**, and **types of predicates**.

                          prep   **op**

Rascal loved holes (of all sizes),

prep   **op**   **inf**

(from crayfish holes) to be explored

prep   **op** **prep** **op**

(with a sensitive paw), (to holes)

                       inf

such as this one, big enough to crawl

dep **sc** **s** **v** **adj** **do** **prep**

into. [While I put fresh straw (in

art **adj** **op** **cc**   **v**   **do** **prep**

the box stall), and enclosed it (in

adj   **op**   **ind adj** **s**   **v**

chicken wire),] [my raccoon spent

adj **prep adj** **op**

most (of his time) going in and out

prep   **op**

(of his pleasant little door).]

Exercises

1. Draw brackets around each clause in the second sentence. Mark any independent clauses with **ind** and any dependent clauses with **dep**. (**dep**: *[While I put fresh straw in the box stall, and enclosed it in chicken wire]*; **ind**: *[my raccoon spent most of his time going in and out of his pleasant little door.]*)

    The first clause has what type of predicate?

    Simple   **⦂Compound⦂**   **Complete**

    Why? *(A compound predicate contains two **verbs** that modify a single **subject**: ...**I put** fresh straw in the box stall, and **enclosed** it in chicken wire...)*

2. Why is there a comma after **chicken wire**?

    ☐ **Because you should always set off parenthetical comments with commas.**

    ☒ **Because you should always set off introductory dependent clauses with commas.**

    ☐ **The comma really isn't necessary.**

    ☐ **Because you should always set off interjections with commas or exclamation points.**

    ☐ **Because you should always set off a nonrestrictive phrase or clause with commas.**

3. Write **inf** above the infinitives. *(to be explored; to crawl)*

4. Underline the word that has a prefix and circle the prefix. *(enclosed)*

5. Analyze the last sentence up to, but not including, the gerund **going**. (**sc**: *While*; **s**: *I*; **v**: *put*; **adj**: *fresh*; **do**: *straw*; **prep**: *in*; **art**: *the*; **adj**: *box*; **op**: *stall*; **cc**: *and*; **v**: *enclosed*; **do**: *it*; **prep**: *in*; **adj**: *chicken*; **op**: *wire*; **adj**: *my*; **s**: *raccoon*; **v**: *spent*; **adj**: *most*; **prep**: *of*; **adj**: *his*; **op**: *time*)

    Mom or Dad: Most functions as an adjective that describes the prepositional phrase (**of his time**).

6. Rewrite the first sentence as two or more sentences. (**Sample answer:** *Rascal loved holes of all sizes. He would use his sensitive paw to explore crayfish-sized holes, and he would crawl right into a hole if it was big enough to accommodate him.*)

7. How many kinds of holes can you think of? See if you can think of six different types of holes. (***Sample answers:*** *hole-in-one; hole-in-the-wall; rabbit hole; pinhole; ice hole; black hole; mouse hole; hole in the head; hidey-hole; etc.*)

Grammar 5: Sheet 49 Answer Guide

Passage

Rascal, pp. 160–161:

Mom or Dad: We highlight **pronouns** on the Activity Sheet. Note the British spelling of catalogues/catalogs.

　　adv　　hv　　　s　　　v　　art
How could anyone mutilate the

　adj　　　　adj　　　n/do　prep art　　n/op
sensitive, questing hands (of an ani-

　prep　　　*/op　　s　　v　　adv adj
mal) (like Rascal)? I picked up my

　n/do　　cc　　v　　　do　prep art　n/op
raccoon and hugged him (in a pas-

　prep　　n/op
sion) (of remorse).

　　　　　　　　　　　　　　n
I burned my fur catalogues in

　　　　n　　　　　　　　　　　n
the furnace and hung my traps in

　　　n　　　　　　　n
the loft of the barn, never to use

　　　　　　　　　n
them again. Men had stopped kill-

　　　n　　　　*　　　　n
ing other men in France that day;

　　　　　　　　　　n
and on that day I signed a perma-

　　　　n　　　　　　　n
nent peace treaty with the animals

　　　n
and the birds. It is perhaps the only

　n
peace treaty that was ever kept.

F.Y.I. Synopsis: More Types of Pronouns

- **Demonstrative pronouns**: point out particular people or things. (There are 4: *this, these, that, those*)

    e.g.　Did you use *this* eraser?

- **Indefinite pronouns**: undefined pronouns. Usually, we don't know exactly to whom or what they refer. (*anyone, someone, most, everyone, everything*, etc.)

    e.g.　Did *anyone* buy milk today?

- **Reflexive pronouns**: refer back to the subject of a sentence. (*myself, yourself, himself, itself*, etc.) **Note:** "hisself" and "theirselves" are not real words!

    e.g.　He tied his shoe *himself*.

- **Intensive pronouns**: exactly the same as reflexive pronouns except used to *emphasize* another noun or pronoun.

    e.g.　My boss *himself* delivered the cookies.

- **Interrogative pronouns**: used in questions.

    Which restaurant shall we visit?[1]

Exercises

1. Write **s** above the simple subject of the first sentence. *(anyone)*

    What kind of word is it?　**An intensive pronoun**
    An indefinite pronoun　**An interrogative pronoun**
    A demonstrative pronoun

2. Write **n** above the nouns and draw asterisks above the proper nouns. *(hands; animal; **Rascal**; raccoon; passion; remorse; catalogues; furnace; traps; loft; barn; Men; men; **France**; day; day; treaty; animals; birds; treaty)*

3. What is the person (first, second, third) and number (singular, plural) of the first word of the second paragraph? *(first person singular)*

4. What is the tense of **men had stopped killing**?
    Simple past　**Continuing past**　**Past perfect**

5. Analyze the first paragraph. **Hint:** The word **How**, here, is an adverb. (**adv:** *How;* **hv:** *could;* **s:** *anyone;* **v:** *mutilate;* **art:** *the;* **adj:** *sensitive;* **part/adj:** *questing;* **do:** *hands;* **prep:** *of;* **art:** *an;* **op:** *animal;* **prep:** *like;* **op:** *Rascal;* **s:** *I;* **v:** *picked;* **adv:** *up;* **pro/adj:** *my;* **do:** *raccoon;* **cc:** *and;* **v:** *hugged;* **do:** *him;* **prep:** *in;* **art:** *a;* **op:** *passion;* **prep:** *of;* **op:** *remorse*)

6. Mr. North used two adjectives to describe the hands of an animal like Rascal. Please come up with at least four other adjectives you might use to describe **hands** (any hands—yours, someone else's, Rascal's, etc.). (***Sample answers:*** *chapped, scaly, clammy, cold, slimy, sweaty, nervous, warm, strong,* etc.)

---

1. See table on today's Activity Sheet.

Grammar 5: Sheet 50 Answer Guide

Passage

Just So Stories, p. 18:

Mom or Dad: We introduce **parallel structure** on today's Activity Sheet. Please discuss the British punctuation—the use of single quotation marks when, in the United States, we would use double quotation marks. Please feel free to utilize the kind of punctuation marks appropriate in your culture!

'Do you see that?' said the Djinn.

ind

['That's <u>your very own</u> humph]

dep

[that you've brought upon <u>your very</u>

                ind **s**

<u>own</u> self by not working]. [Today

lv   **pn**   **ind cc** **s** **hv** **v** **adj**

is Thursday], [and you've done no

  do   **prep**   **op**   **dep** **sc**   **art**

work (since Monday)], [when the

  s   **v**

work began]. Now you are going to

work.'

F.Y.I.: Parallel Structure

A sentence contains **parallel structure** when the same pattern of words is used repeatedly to show that multiple ideas have the same level of importance. Usually, <u>coordinating conjunctions</u> join parallel structures. For example:

> Austin likes *to hike, to swim,* <u>and</u> *to play* hockey.

Parallel structure can also appear as clauses:

> Our youth pastor told us *that we should* get plenty of rest, *that we should* bring a sack lunch, <u>and</u> *that we should* leave our headphones at home on the day we left for our trip.

In order for the structure to be parallel, all elements must stay in the same form. Here are a few examples that are not parallel, due to the change in form.

> Please finish the test quick*ly*, accurate*ly*, and ***in the required amount of time***.

> In my swimming class, you will learn breath*ing*, kick*ing*, pull*ing* and ***proper stroke techniques***.

Exercises

1. Find the parallel expression in the second sentence. Please underline both halves of the parallelism. *(your very own—your very own)*

   Why do you think the Djinn uses the parallelism? *(to emphasize that the camel was personally responsible for his own personal condition)*

2. Draw brackets around each clause in the second sentence. Mark any independent clauses with **ind** and any dependent clauses with **dep**. *(**ind:** [That's your very own humph]; **dep:** [that you've brought upon your very own self by not working])*

   Therefore, what is the structure of this sentence?

   Simple Compound (Complex) **Compound-Complex**

3. Draw brackets around each clause in the third sentence. Mark any independent clauses with **ind** and any dependent clauses with **dep**. *(**ind:** [Today is Thursday], [and you've done no work since Monday]; **dep:** [when the work began])*

   Therefore, what is the structure of this sentence?

   Simple Compound Complex (Compound-Complex)

4. What type of sentence is the first quoted sentence?

   Imperative (Interrogative) **Exclamatory Declarative**

   What type of sentence is the last one?

   Imperative Interrogative Exclamatory (Declarative)

5. The gerund **working** is a noun. What is its grammatical function? *(working is the object of the preposition by; only nouns can act as objects of prepositions)*

6. Analyze the third sentence. *(**s:** Today; **lv:** is; **pn:** Thursday; **cc:** and; **s:** you; **hv:** [ha]ve; **v:** done; **adj:** no; **do:** work; **prep:** since; **op:** Monday; **sc:** when; **art:** the; **s:** work; **v:** began)*

Grammar 5: Sheet 51 Answer Guide

Passage

Just So Stories, p. 111:

Mom or Dad: Please review **hyphens**, **roots** and **suffixes**. **Note:** We're not sure why Kipling has the comma and the dash in the phrase **twenty-six of 'em,—and**.... It would be better to simply provide the comma and not furnish a second dash.

Some day men will call it <u>writing</u>.

prep **op** **s** **lv** **adj** **pn** **cc**
(At present) it is only <u>pictures</u>, and,

sc **s** **hv** **v** **adv** **s** **hv**
as we have <u>seen</u> today, <u>pictures</u> are

adv **adv** **adv** **v**
not always <u>properly</u> understood. But

nda
a time will come, O Babe of Tegu-

mai, when we shall make <u>letters</u>—

appos
(all twenty-six of 'em),—and when

inf **inf**
we shall be able to read as well as to

write, and then we shall always say

<u>exactly</u> what we mean without any

<u>mistakes</u>.

Exercises

1. Draw an arrow that points to the hyphen. What is it used for?
   - ☐ **To form an adjective**
   - ☐ **To create a compound word**
   - ☐ **To show that something is missing**
   - ☐ **To avoid confusion or awkward spelling**
   - ☐ **To create a new word**
   - ☒ **To create a compound number between twenty-one and ninety-nine**
   - ☐ **There is no good reason to include a hyphen**

2. Draw parentheses around and write **appos** above the appositive phrase. *(all twenty-six of 'em)*

3. Write **inf** above any infinitives. *(to read; to write)*

4. Write **nda** above the noun of direct address. *([O] Babe of Tegumai)*

5. Underline any words that have suffixes. Write the original root words here: *(writing—write; pictures—picture; seen—see; pictures—picture; properly—proper; letters—letter; exactly—exact; mistakes—mistake)*

6. **Challenge: Men** and **understood** have been modified without suffixes. Write their root words here: *(Man, understand)*

7. What is the tense of the first sentence?
   Past   **Present**   ⟨**Future**⟩

8. What is the structure of the first sentence?
   ⟨**Simple**⟩ **Compound** **Complex** **Compound-Complex**
   What is the structure of the second sentence?
   Simple **Compound** **Complex** ⟨**Compound-Complex**⟩
   What is the structure of the third sentence?
   Simple **Compound** **Complex** ⟨**Compound-Complex**⟩

9. Analyze the second sentence. (**prep:** *At;* **op:** *present;* **s:** *it;* **lv:** *is;* **adj:** *only;* **pn:** *pictures;* **cc:** *and;* **sc:** *as;* **s:** *we;* **hv:** *have;* **v:** *seen;* **adv:** *today;* **s:** *pictures;* **hv:** *are;* **adv:** *not;* **adv:** *always;* **adv:** *properly;* **v:** *understood*)

10. The author wrote the last clause in the second sentence in the passive voice. Please rewrite it in the active voice. (**Sample answer:** *People don't always understand pictures.*)

Grammar 5: Sheet 52 Answer Guide

Passage

Just So Stories, p. 177:

Mom or Dad: Please review **pronoun case**. We introduce **interjections** on today's Activity Sheet.

    ind int   v   art   s   part/adj
["Ah," said the Woman, listening],

ind s   lv art adv   adj   pn *ind* cc s lv
["this is a very clever Cat], [but he is

  adv adv pa
not so clever as my Man]."

F.Y.I.: Interjections

An **interjection** is a one- or two-word expression of strong emotion or surprise. Interjections often end with an exclamation point, or may be set apart from the rest of a sentence with commas.

> *Ah,* how I love summertime.
> *Wow!* Is that the score of the game?
> *Oh!* Would you also pick up dessert on your way home?

Exercises

1. Write **int** above the interjection and **part/adj** above the participle. *(int: Ah;* **part:** *listening)*

2. Draw an arrow from **he** to its antecedent. *(he—Cat)*

3. Draw brackets around each clause. Mark any independent clauses with **ind** and any dependent clauses with **dep**. *(ind: ["Ah," said the Woman, listening]; ind: [this is a very clever Cat]; ind: [but he is not so clever as my Man])*

Therefore, what is its sentence structure?

Simple ⟨Compound⟩ Complex Compound-Complex

4. In the last clause, what is the case of the pronoun **he**?

⟨Nominative⟩ Possessive Objective

5. Analyze the sentence up to, but not including, **as my Man**. **Note:** the participle serves as an adjective to describe the **Woman**. *(int: Ah;* **v:** *said;* **art:** *the;* **s:** *Woman;* **part/adj:** *listening;* **s:** *this;* **lv:** *is;* **art:** *a;* **adv:** *very;* **adj:** *clever;* **pn:** *Cat;* **cc:** *but;* **s:** *he;* **lv:** *is;* **adv:** *not;* **adv:** *so;* **pa:** *clever)*

6. Rewrite the sentence in such a way that the attribution comes in a different spot. ***(Sample answers:** "Ah! This is a very clever Cat," said the Woman, listening. "But he is not so clever as my Man." –OR– "Ah! This is a very clever Cat, but he is not so clever as my Man," said the Woman, listening. –OR– The Woman, listening, said, "Ah! This is a very clever Cat. But he is not so clever as my Man.")*

7. Write synonyms for the following words. Of course you may use prepositional phrases or participles if they work! ***(Sample answers:** **said** spoke, mentioned, stated; **listening** taking notice, observing, hanging on every word; **very** extremely, most, astonishingly; **clever** smart, brilliant, sly)*

Grammar 5: Sheet 53 Answer Guide

Passage

Around the World in Eighty Days, p. 14:

Mom or Dad: Please review **similes**, and **reflexive** and **intensive pronouns**. Also note that we have modified our passage to follow American rather than British punctuation standards.

<pre>
  int/prep adj   op   v   s
</pre>
"(Upon my word)," said Passepar-
<pre>
  prep   op   s   hv   v   prep
</pre>
tout (to himself), "I have known (<u>at</u>
<pre>
    op   adj   do
</pre>
<u>Madame Tussaud's) good people as</u>
<u>lively as my new master!"</u>

It is proper to say here that Madame Tussaud's "good people" are wax figures, much visited in London, and who, indeed, are only wanting in speech.

Exercises

1. Write **int** above the interjection. *(Upon my word)* Write two new interjections. (**Sample answers:** *Unbelievable! Yuck! Good grief!)*

2. Underline the simile in today's passage. *(at madame Tussaud's good people as lively as my new master)*

3. Passepartout, we are told, speaks **to himself**. Depending on the context in which it is used, **himself** is a reflexive or intensive pronoun. Which is it here?
   Reflexive   Intensive
   Suppose Passepartout had said, **I myself have known at Madame Tussaud's good people as lively as my new master!** Would **myself**, in that context, be a reflexive or intensive pronoun?
   Reflexive   **Intensive**
   Write four other reflexive or intensive pronouns (other than **himself** and **myself**). (**Sample answers:** *herself, themselves, itself, ourselves)*

4. **Visited** and **wanting** are participles. Rewrite the last clause to replace these participles with verbs. (**Sample answer:** *Many people visit them in London. They only lack speech.)*

5. Analyze the first sentence up to, but not including, **as lively as my new master**. (**prep:** *Upon;* **adj:** *my;* **op:** *word;* **v:** *said;* **s:** *Passepartout;* **prep:** *to;* **op:** *himself;* **s:** *I;* **hv:** *have;* **v:** *known;* **prep:** *at;* **op:** *Madame Tussaud's;* **adj:** *good;* **do:** *people)*

6. According to the passage, what is the only thing the wax figurines at Madame Tussaud's lack? *(they cannot speak)*

Grammar 5: Sheet 54 Answer Guide

Passage

Around the World in Eighty Days, p. 24:

Mom or Dad: Please review **sentence fragments** and **parenthetical expressions**. Surprisingly, the lowercase **but** is not an error. It is possible to conclude an interjection with an exclamation point and continue the ongoing sentence with a lowercase letter.

int   s   v   do   v

"Heaven preserve me!" exclaimed

s   cc   s   hv   adv   v

Stuart, "but I would willingly wager

adj   do   sc   adj   art

four thousand pounds that such a

s   part/adj   prep   adj   op

journey, [made under these condi-

lv   pa

tions], is impossible."

int

"<u>On the contrary, quite possible</u>,"

replied Mr. Fogg.

int

"Well, make it, then!"

"<u>The tour of the world in eighty</u>

<u>days</u>?"

"<u>Yes</u>!"

"I am willing."

Exercises

1. Write **int** above any interjections and put brackets around the parenthetical expression. *(*int: *Heaven preserve me!;* int: *On the contrary;* int: *Well;* parenthetical: *made under these conditions)*

2. Find and write all words that have prefixes or suffixes, then rewrite them in their root forms. *(preserve—serve; exclaimed–claim; willingly–will; pounds–pound; conditions–condition; impossible–possible; replied–reply; eighty–eight; days–day; willing–will)*

3. Underline the three sentence fragments. *(On the contrary, quite possible; The tour of the world in eighty days?; Yes!)*

4. Write the sentence fragments as complete sentences. *(**Sample answers:** On the contrary; it is quite possible. –Also– You want me to make the tour of the world in eighty days?)*

5. Think of two antonyms or, at least, contrastive expressions for each of the following words. Feel free to use prepositional phrases, clauses, or other longer means of expressing the opposite idea! *(**Sample answers:** **heaven** hell, under world, Hades; **preserve** destroy, wreck, knock down; **under** over, on top of, above; **contrary** the same, in favor, in agreement; **wager** risk nothing, hold tight; **impossible** possible, likely, almost certain, easy)*

6. Analyze the first sentence. **Hint:** The word **made** is a participle. *(**s:** Heaven; **v:** preserve; **do:** me; **v:** exclaimed; **s:** Stuart; **cc:** but; **s:** I; **hv:** would; **adv:** willingly; **v:** wager; **adj:** four thousand; **do:** pounds; **sc:** that; **adj:** such; **art:** a; **s:** journey; **part/adj:** made; **prep:** under; **adj:** these; **op:** conditions; **lv:** is; **pa:** impossible)*

Grammar 5: Sheet 55 Answer Guide

Passage

Around the World in Eighty Days, pp. 51–52:

Mom or Dad: Please review **participles**. You should probably note that the current population of India is over one billion people!

| adj | s | lv | pa | prep | art | op |

No one is ignorant (of the fact)

part

that India, <u>this great reversed trian-</u>

prep **op**

<u>gle whose base is (to the north) and</u>

prep **op**

<u>its apex (to the south)</u>, comprises a

prep

superficial area (of fourteen hundred

op **prep** **op**

thousand square miles), (over which)

part

is unequally scattered a population

prep **op**

(of one hundred and eighty millions)

prep **op**

(of inhabitants).

Exercises

1. Write **prep** above all prepositions, **op** above all objects of prepositions, and draw parentheses around all prepositional phrases. *(of the **fact**; to the **north**; to the **south**; of fourteen hundred thousand square **miles**; over **which**; of one hundred and eighty **millions**; of **inhabitants**)*

2. Write **part** above the participles **reversed** and **scattered**. Draw arrows to the nouns they modify. *(reversed—triangle; scattered—population)*

3. Underline the appositive phrase. *(this great reversed triangle whose base is to the north and its apex to the south)*

4. Write a homophone for each of the following words. **(great** *<u>grate</u>;* **one** *<u>won</u>;* **whose** *<u>who's</u>;* **its** *<u>it's</u>;* **eight** *<u>ate</u>;* **which** *<u>witch</u>)*

5. Analyze the clause **No one is ignorant of the fact**. If you find a prepositional phrase, please surround it with parentheses. **(adj:** *No;* **s:** *one;* **lv:** *is;* **pa:** *ignorant;* **prep:** *of;* **art:** *the;* **op:** *fact;* **prep phrase:** *(of the fact))*

6. Describe the same triangle in your own words. *(an upside-down triangle whose point faces down)*

Grammar 5: Sheet 56 Answer Guide

Passage

Around the World in Eighty Days, p. 71:

Mom or Dad: Please review **capitalization**. We discuss **attributions** on the Activity Sheet.

art   n/s   n/nda   v   art
"A suttee, Mr. Fogg," replied the

n/s   lv art   adj
brigadier-gen/er/al, "is a hu/man

n/pn   cc   art   adj   n/pn
sacrifice, but a vol/un/tar/y sac/ri/

art   n/s   sc   s   hv   adv
fice. The wo/man that you have just

v   hv   hv   v   adv   prep
seen will be burned to/mor/row (in

art   adj   n/op   prep art   n/op
the ear/ly part) (of the day)."

F.Y.I.: Attribution

You probably already know that an **attribution** is the phrase that indicates who said whatever is being quoted. Attributions can be placed before, in the middle of, or after a quotation. Let's discuss some of the nuances of attributions to help you write them correctly.

When the attribution appears before a quotation, name the speaker, follow that with a comma, and then state the quotation.

> *Bo said,* "Where shall we go for lunch?"

When the attribution lies in the middle of a sentence, we set the attribution off with commas.

> "I emailed the file to you," *said Duane,* "and will put the books in the mail today."

When the attribution falls between two sentences of a quote, attach the attribution to the sentence that comes before it, and separate it with a comma. **Note:** the comma should lie on the inside of the closing quotation mark.

> "Here is a box for you," *said Nate.* "I can help you carry it to your car if you like."

Keep in mind that if the quoted sentence ends in an exclamation point or a question mark, keep them—don't replace them with a comma.

> "That's the best thing I've heard in a long time!" *exclaimed Duane.*
> "Can you believe it?" *Amber asked.*

Finally, you should start a new paragraph whenever a new speaker begins to talk in a dialog. Once you have identified the characters, however, you don't have to include attributions in every line. The change in paragraphs is enough for the reader to understand that two characters are speaking back and forth.

> "Is that dinosaur going to eat us?" *gasped Amber.*
> "No," *sighed Bubba,* "That's a friendly one."
> "How can you tell?"
> "He's wearing a name tag."

Exercises

1. Rewrite the first sentence so that the attribution moves and the quotation itself is simpler. *(**Sample answer:** The brigadier-general replied, "A suttee, Mr. Fogg, is a voluntary human sacrifice.)*

2. Write **n** above the nouns. *(suttee, Mr. Fogg, brigadier-general, sacrifice, sacrifice, woman, part, day)*

3. Use slashes to divide **general, human, sacrifice, voluntary, woman, tomorrow,** and **early** into syllables. *(gen/er/al; hu/man; vol/un/tar/y; sac/ri/fice; wo/man; to/mor/row; ear/ly)*

4. What is the tense of the verb **replied** in the first sentence?

   Past Perfect ⟨Past⟩ **Present Perfect Present**

   What is the tense of the verb phrase **have just seen**?

   Past Perfect ⟨Present Perfect⟩ **Present Future**

   What is the tense of the verb phrase **will be burned**?

   Past Past Perfect Present ⟨Future⟩

5. Analyze the paragraph. *(**art:** A; **s:** suttee; **nda:** Mr. Fogg; **v:** replied; **art:** the; **s:** brigadier-general; **lv:** is; **art:** a; **adj:** human; **pn:** sacrifice; **cc:** but; **art:** a; **adj:** voluntary; **pn:** sacrifice; **art:** The; **s:** woman; **sc:** that; **s:** you; **hv:** have; **adv:** just; **v:** seen; **hv:** will; **hv:** be; **v:** burned; **adv:** tomorrow; **prep:** in; **art:** the; **adj:** early; **op:** part; **prep:** of; **art:** the; **op:** day)*

6. Write a sentence in which **brigadier-general** should be capitalized. *(Any sentence where Brigadier-General is used as a title. **For example:** Brigadier-General Smith inspected the troops.)*

Grammar 5: Sheet 57 Answer Guide

Passage

Around the World in Eighty Days, p. 86:

Mom or Dad: Please review **parenthetical expressions**. If you use these passages for dictation, please end today's dictation immediately before the first dash (i.e., right after the word lost).

          ^{prep}   ^{op}
(According to his journal), this

gentleman should arrive (in the capital) (of India), October 25, twenty-
three days (after leaving) London,
and he arrived there (on the stipulated day). He was neither behind
nor ahead (of time). Unfortunately,
the two days gained (by him)
(between London and Bombay) had
been lost—we know how—(in this
trip) (across the Indian peninsula),
but it is to be supposed that Phileas
Fogg did not regret them.

Exercises

1. Write **prep** above all prepositions, **op** above all objects of prepositions, and draw parentheses around all prepositional phrases. *(according to his **journal**; in the capital; of India; after leaving; on the stipulated **day**; of time; by him; between London and Bombay; in this trip; across the Indian peninsula)*

2. Write **part** above the participles **stipulated** and **gained**, and draw arrows from the participles to the nouns or pronouns they modify. *(stipulated—day; gained—days)*

   The word **leaving** is what? (Check all that apply)

   ☐ **A participle**
   ☒ **A gerund**
   ☐ **A direct object**
   ☐ **A predicate adjective**
   ☒ **An object of a preposition**
   ☒ **A noun**

3. Draw an arrow that points to the hyphen.

   What is the hyphen used for? (Check all that apply.)

   ☐ **To form an adjective**
   ☐ **To create a compound word**
   ☐ **To show that something is missing**
   ☐ **To avoid confusion or awkward spelling**
   ☒ **To create a number between twenty-one and ninety-nine**
   ☐ **There is no good reason to include a hyphen**

4. Circle the one word that has a prefix and a suffix. Write the root of this word here: *(fortune)*

5. Analyze the last clause from the subordinating conjunction **that**. *(**sc:** that; **s:** Phileas Fogg; **hv:** did; **adv:** not; **v:** regret; **do:** them)*

6. Draw a box around the parenthetical expression. *(we know how)*

   How else might the parenthetical expression be punctuated? *(**Best answer:** parentheses; one can also use commas, though we don't recommend it here as the phrase is too long for commas)*

7. Write at least three other ways you might communicate the meaning of the phrase **the stipulated day**.

   *(**Sample answers:** the set day, the agreed-upon day, the appointed day, the designated day)*

Grammar 5: Sheet 58 Answer Guide

Passage

Around the World in Eighty Days, pp. 106–107:

Mom or Dad: Today we introduce **italics**.

prep   op   prep   op

(During the days) (of the third

op   prep   op

and fourth) (of November) it was a

prep   op   art   s   v

sort (of tempest). <u>The squall struck</u>

art   do   prep   op   art   s

<u>the sea (with violence).</u> The *Rangoon*

v   inf   adv   prep adj art op

had to go slowly (for half a day),

part   prep   op   prep

<u>keeping herself (in motion)</u> (with

adv   adj   op   prep art   op

only ten revolutions) (of the screw),

inf   prep   op

<u>so as to lean (with the waves).</u> All

the sails had been reefed, and there

part

was still too much <u>rigging whistling</u>

prep   op

<u>(in the squall).</u>

F.Y.I.: Italics

In printed materials, **italic type** (which looks slightly slanted *like this*) is used in a number of ways.

Italics can identify titles of books, magazines and album titles.

Pride and Prejudice is the next book I plan to read.

Let's order *Reader's Digest* for Grandma.

The Dave Matthews Band song "Ants Marching" is on the album *Under the Table and Dreaming.*

Italics are also used to give emphasis to a particular word or phrase.

She was *really* excited to see me.

Italics can also identify words that are being used or discussed somehow.

The phrase *so that* is a subordinating conjunction.

Finally, italics can help identify foreign words.

I only had three *pesos* left after our trip to the market.

Exercises

1. Why is **Rangoon** italicized?
   - [ ] **It is a parenthetical expression**
   - [x] **It is the name of the boat**
   - [ ] **For emphasis**

2. Write **prep** above all prepositions, **op** above all objects of prepositions, and draw parentheses around all prepositional phrases.[1] *(During* the **days**; *of* the **third** and **fourth**; *of* **November**; *of* **tempest**; *with* **violence**; *for* half a **day**; *in* **motion**; *with* only ten **revolutions**; *of* the **screw**; *with* the **waves**; *in* the **squall**)

3. Write **inf** above any infinitives. *(to go; to lean)*

4. Underline the personification in the passage. *(**Possible:** The squall struck the sea with violence; keeping herself in motion; so as to lean with the waves; rigging whistling in the squall)*

5. Analyze the second sentence and the third sentence through the word **screw**. **Hint:** Treat the words **had to go** as a single verb phrase; mark it, therefore, as **v**. Skip the phrase **keeping herself**, and remember: adverbs modify adjectives. *(**art:** The; **s:** squall; **v:** struck; **art:** the; **do:** sea; **prep:** with; **op:** violence; **art:** The; **s:** Rangoon; **v:** had to go; **adv:** slowly; **prep:** for; **adj:** half; **art:** a; **op:** day; **prep:** in; **op:** motion; **prep:** with; **adv:** only; **adj:** ten; **op:** revolutions; **prep:** of; **art:** the; **op:** screw)*

6. Write **part** above the participles **keeping** and **whistling**. Draw arrows from the participles or participial phrases to the nouns they modify. *(keeping—herself; whistling—rigging)*

7. Rewrite the last sentence and replace the participle **whistling** with a true verb. *(**Sample answer:** All the sails had been reefed, but there was still too much rigging. The rigging whistled in the squall.)*

---

1. **Mom or Dad:** Formal grammarians may consider the word "of" to be an "understood" preposition in the phrase **for half** [of] **a day**. If so, it would mean that instead of **half** serving as an adjective to modify **day** (as it does in our answer), the prepositional phrase [of] **a day** would serve as an adjective that modifies **half**. Regardless, please keep in mind that at the elementary grade levels, we ought to ignore such fine points! We ought to be delighted that our kids can simply identify prepositions.

Grammar 5: Sheet 59 Answer Guide

Passage

Around the World in Eighty Days, p. 126:

    adj   s   prep   adj

This voyage (of eight hundred

op   *part*   part/adj   prep art op

miles), [undertaken (in a craft)

prep adj   op   cc   adv

(of twenty tons)], and especially

prep adj   op   prep art op   lv

(in that season) (of the year), was

    pa

venturesome. The Chinese seas

    part   prep

are generally rough, [exposed (to

    op   prep

terrible blows)], principally (during

  op   prep

the equinoxes), and this was (in the

    op   prep   op

first days) (of November).

Exercises

1. Analyze the first sentence. If you find a prepositional phrase, please surround it with parentheses. **Note: undertaken** is a participle acting as an adjective. (**adj**: *This;* **s**: *voyage;* **prep**: *of;* **adj**: *eight hundred;* **op**: *miles;* **prep phrase**: *(of eight hundred miles);* **part/adj**: *undertaken;* **prep**: *in;* **art**: *a;* **op**: *craft;* **prep phrase**: *(in a craft);* **prep**: *of;* **adj**: *twenty;* **op**: *tons;* **prep phrase**: *(of twenty tons);* **cc**: *and;* **adv**: *especially;* **prep**: *in;* **adj**: *that;* **op**: *season;* **prep phrase**: *(in that season);* **prep**: *of;* **art**: *the;* **op**: *year;* **prep phrase**: *(of the year);* **lv**: *was;* **pa**: *venturesome)*

2. Draw brackets around and write **part** above the participial phrases, **undertaken in a craft of twenty tons** and **exposed to terrible blows**. Draw an arrow to the nouns or pronouns they modify. **(undertaken in a…— voyage; exposed to…—seas)**

3. Write the root words of the following: **(miles** *mile;* **especially** *special;* **generally** *general;* **exposed** *expose;* **principally** *principal;* **equinoxes** *equinox)*

4. Rewrite the first sentence in its simplest form (with all of the prepositions, prepositional phrases, and participial phrases removed). (***Sample answer:*** *This voyage was venturesome.*)

5. The following words are all homographs. Write one additional meaning for each word. (***Sample answers:*** **blows** *wind storms; strikes or hits;* **rough** *choppy, hard to navigate; long grass at the edge of a golf course; harsh; violent;* **exposed** *at risk; to make subject to the action of something (as film to light);* **craft** *ship, boat; an art project)*

6. What adjectives could you use to communicate the idea contained in the word **venturesome**? List at least four. (***Sample answers:*** *interesting, ambitious, risky, dangerous, wild, exciting, difficult, etc.)*

7. What is the difference between **a principal** and **a principle**? (**a principal:** *first, highest or foremost— either as an adjective or a noun; a person who is in charge at a school;* **a principle:** *a basic truth or law)*

8. **Challenge:** What are the equinoxes? *(the two days in the year when daylight lasts for 12 hours; when day and night are equal in length)*
   When are the equinoxes? *(vernal (i.e., spring): March 20/21; autumnal (i.e., fall): September 21)*
   So how significant is the information that **this was in the first days of November**? *(it means it was still a stormy time of year)*

9. **Challenge:** How many pounds is twenty tons, if a ton is 2,000 pounds? *(40,000 pounds; there are 2,000 pounds in a ton)*

Grammar 5: Sheet 60 Answer Guide

Passage

Around the World in Eighty Days, p. 155:

Mom or Dad: Please review **rhyme**.

   ind   *ind*

["Now," continued Fix], "[Mr. Fogg

       inf

seems to be returning to England?]

ind *int* *s* *hv* *v* *do* *adv* *ind*

[Well, I will follow him there.] [But

                inf

hence/forth it shall be my aim to

clear the obstacles from his path]

dep

[as zealously and carefully as before

               inf

I took pains to accumulate them].

ind *int* *adj* *s* *lv* *part/pa* *ind* *cc*

[You see, my game is changed], [and

s *lv* *part/pa* *dep* *sc* *adj* *s*

it is changed] [because my interest

    v   *do*

desires it]."

Exercises

1. Write **inf** above the infinitives. *(to be, to clear, to accumulate)*

2. Draw brackets around each clause. Mark any independent clauses with **ind** and any dependent clauses with **dep**. *(**ind:** ['Now,' continued Fix]; **ind:** [Mr. Fogg seems to be returning to England?]; **ind:** [Well, I will follow him there]; **ind:** [But henceforth it shall be my aim to clear the obstacles from his path]; **dep:** [as zealously and carefully as before I took pains to accumulate them]; **ind:** [You see my game is changed]; **ind:** [and it is changed]; **dep:** [because my interest desires it])*

3. Based on your analysis, what is the structure of the first sentence?

   Simple **Compound** Complex Compound-Complex

   What is the structure of the second?

   Simple Compound Complex Compound-Complex

   What is the structure of the third?

   Simple Compound **Complex** Compound-Complex

   What is the structure of the fourth?

   Simple Compound Complex **Compound-Complex**

4. Put boxes around any compound words, then use slashes to divide them into their parts. *(hence/forth)*

5. The author (actually, translator) forgot to punctuate one of the interjections the way it should be. Please add the appropriate punctuation and circle it. *(You see,)*

6. Analyze the second and fourth sentences. **Hint:** The word **changed** is a participle. *(**int:** Well; **s:** I; **hv:** will; **v:** follow; **do:** him; **adv:** there; **int:** You see; **adj:** my; **s:** game; **lv:** is; **part/pa:** changed; **cc:** and; **s:** it; **lv:** is; **part/pa:** changed; **sc:** because; **adj:** my; **s:** interest; **v:** desires; **do:** it)*

7. What is the grammatical term for words like **Now**, **Well**, and **You see** as they are used in today's dictation?

   Exclamation   Declaration   **Interjection**
   Dejection   Superlative

8. Fix uses two words that rhyme: **aim** and **game**. Write at least five more words that rhyme with these two. Try to include at least one each that uses the same spelling pattern as each of the two pattern words. *(**Sample answers:** lame, same, name, dame, fame, claim, maim, shame...)*

Grammar 5: Sheet 61 Answer Guide

Passage

Around the World in Eighty Days, p. 195:

Mom or Dad: We introduce **alphabetization** on today's Activity Sheet.

       n   **prep**

Mrs. Aouda retired (into a sit-

  n/op   **prep**   **n/op**

ting room) (of the station), and

                          prep

there, alone, she waited, thinking (of

   n/op

Phileas Fogg, his simple and grand

  n/op   **n/op**   **n**

generosity, his quiet courage). Mr.

                  n

Fogg had sacrificed his fortune, and

               n

now he was staking his life—and all

    prep   **n/op**   **prep**

this (with/out hesitation), (from a

 n/op   **prep n/op**   **prep**   **n/op**

sense) (of duty), (with/out words).

    n/s   **lv** **art n/pn** **prep adj**

Phileas Fogg was a hero (in her

  n/op

eyes).

F.Y.I.: Alphabetization

How many things can you think of that are in alphabetical order? Dictionaries, phone books, indices and books in a library are just some of the things that are alphabetized. Once you get a firm grip on how to **alphabetize** lists, it will help you find information in many places more quickly.

Alphabetization is the process of putting a series of words in alphabetical order (from *a* to *z*) according to the first letter of each word. If multiple words start with the same letter, compare the second letters or third letters... until you find letters that are different, and then order the words accordingly.

this	these	those	that	ours
ours	that	these	this	those

Exercises

1. Alphabetize the words in the last sentence. *(a, eyes, Fogg, her, hero, in, Phileas, was)*

2. Write **n** above the nouns. *(Mrs. Aouda, room, station, Phileas Fogg, generosity, courage, Mr. Fogg, fortune, life, hesitation, sense, duty, words, Phileas Fogg, hero, eyes)*

3. Write **prep** above all prepositions, **op** above all objects of prepositions, and draw parentheses around all prepositional phrases. *(into* a sitting ***room***; *of* the ***station***; *of* ***Phileas Fogg***, *his* simple and grand ***generosity***, *his* quiet ***courage***; *without* ***hesitation***; *from* a ***sense***; *of* ***duty***; *without* ***words***; *in* her ***eyes***)*

4. Put boxes around the compound words and use slashes to divide them into the words of which they are made. *(with/out; with/out)*

5. What is the case of **she**, the first pronoun in the passage?

   Nominative　Objective　Possessive

   What is the case of **his**, the first pronoun in the second sentence?

   Nominative　Objective　**Possessive**

6. What is the tense of the first clause in the second sentence?

   Past Perfect　Simple Past　Continuing Present

   What is the tense of the second clause in the same sentence?　**Simple present**

   Continuing Past　Continuing Present

7. Why did the author use a dash?

   ☒ **To set off a parenthetical or explanatory remark**

   ☐ **To indicate interrupted speech**

   ☐ **To emphasize the words that follow**

   ☐ **It doesn't belong there; the author should have used _____ instead**

8. Analyze the last sentence. (**s:** *Phileas Fogg;* **lv:** *was;* **art:** *a;* **pn:** *hero;* **prep:** *in;* **adj:** *her;* **op:** *eyes*)

Grammar 5: Sheet 62 Answer Guide

Passage

Ali and the Golden Eagle, p. 12:

Mom or Dad: Please review **pronouns** and **antecedents**.

Their houses were hundreds (of
years) old, built and rebuilt (from
mud bricks) (with straw) to hold
them together. The stones lining
the street were worn down (from
centuries) (of being walked on).
The villagers had burros, sheep,
and goats, and all were healthy and
well fed. Almost everything was
made (by hand) (from the natural
resources) found (in their isolated
valley).

Exercises

1. Write **prep** above all prepositions, **op** above all objects of prepositions, and draw parentheses around all prepositional phrases. *(of years; from mud bricks; with straw; from centuries; of being walked on; by hand; from the natural resources; in their isolated valley)*

2. Write **part** above the participles **built, rebuilt, lining, fed,** and **found.** Draw arrows that point from these participles to the nouns for which they serve as adjectives. *(built—houses; rebuilt—houses; lining—stones; fed—all; found—resources)*

3. Analyze the third sentence. (**art:** *The;* **s:** *villagers;* **v:** *had;* **do:** *burros;* **do:** *sheep;* **cc:** *and;* **do:** *goats;* **cc:** *and;* **s:** *all;* **lv:** *were;* **pa:** *healthy;* **cc:** *and;* **adv:** *well;* **part/pa:** *fed)*

4. Rewrite the second sentence in the active voice. *(**Sample answer:** The villagers had worn down the stones in the streets by walking on them year after year down through the centuries.)*

5. Mr. Grover did not write very clearly when he said the houses were **built and rebuilt from mud bricks with straw to hold *them* together.** ...to which noun does the pronoun **them** refer: the **houses** or the **bricks**? Does the straw hold the mud bricks together, or does the straw hold the houses together? Really, it makes more sense that the straw held the mud in the bricks together. Please rewrite the first sentence in such a way that you eliminate this ambiguity. *(**Sample answers:** Their houses were hundreds of years old. They had been built and rebuilt from bricks made of mud and straw. The straw held the mud bricks together.)*

6. Is the first sentence a good topic sentence?
   - ☐ **Yes**
   - ☐ **Another would be better**
   - ☒ **There really isn't a good topic sentence in the paragraph**

   Why? (Discuss your answer with your mom or dad.)

   Mom or Dad: Though all the sentences help to describe the village, none of them really summarizes what all of them are about! Each sentence touches on a different aspect of the subject as a whole.

7. **Challenge:** What grammatical function does the gerund clause **being walked on** fulfill? *(it serves as the object of a preposition (**of**) so it must be functioning as a noun)*

Grammar 5: Sheet 63 Answer Guide

Passage

Ali and the Golden Eagle, p. 44:

Mom or Dad: Please review **helping verbs**.

ind/nda   s   v   art   do   prep   op
[Ali, I have a surprise (for you)].

ind   hv   inf
[Today we will build a way to catch

ind/s   v   do
an eagle baby]. [I have everything

s   v   prep adj   op   *ind*
we need (in my Rover)]. [Come],

ind hv   inf
[we have much work to do].

Exercises

1. Write **nda** above the noun of direct address. *(Ali)*

2. Draw brackets around each clause. Mark any independent clauses with **ind** and any dependent clauses with **dep**. *(**ind:** [Ali, I have a surprise for you]; **ind:** [Today we will build a way to catch an eagle baby]; **ind:** [I have everything we need in my Rover]; **ind:** [Come]; **ind:** [we have much work to do])*

3. Based on your analysis, what is the structure of the first sentence?
   Simple Compound Complex Compound-Complex

What is the structure of the second?
Simple Compound Complex Compound-Complex

What is the structure of the third?
Simple Compound Complex Compound-Complex

What is the structure of the fourth?
Simple **Compound** Complex Compound-Complex

4. Write **inf** above any infinitives. *(to catch, to do)*

5. Write **hv** over the helping verb(s). *(will, have)*

6. Analyze the first and third sentences. *(**nda:** Ali; **s:** I; **v:** have; **art:** a; **do:** surprise; **prep:** for; **op:** you; **s:** I; **v:** have; **do:** everything; **s:** we; **v:** need; **prep:** in; **adj:** my; **op:** Rover)*

7. Write at least four adverbs to describe the verb **work**. *(**Sample answers:** slowly, forever, like a dog, like a beaver, in the dark…)*

8. Why is **Rover** capitalized? *(because it is a proper noun—the name of the type of vehicle Mr. Grover was driving)*

9. Mr. Grover said that he and Ali had **much** work to do. Write at least four other adjectives (or adjectival phrases) for the noun **work**. *(**Sample answers:** hard, back-breaking, easy, sweaty, exhilarating, enjoyable, satisfying)*

Grammar 5: Sheet 64 Answer Guide

Passage

Ali and the Golden Eagle, p. 72:

Mom or Dad: Please review the difference between **homonyms** and **homographs**, as well as **parallel structure** and **expletives**.

dep/nda sc s   hv   v   adj   do
[Ali, if we can master this bird],

ind/s hv v   art   adj   do
[we will have the greatest hunter

prep adj   op   adv   prep adj art
(in all Arabia), perhaps (in all the

op   *ind*/exp   lv art adj   s   pa
world)]. [There is a long road ahead],

ind/cc s   hv   v   do   adv
[but we will take it together].

Exercises

1. As it is used in the second sentence, what is the grammatical function of **There**? Be careful!

   A subject   An object   An adverb   An expletive

2. Analyze the paragraph. **Hint:** Use your answer to Question 1 to help you analyze the first clause of the second sentence. **(nda:** *Ali;* **sc:** *if;* **s:** *we;* **hv:** *can;* **v:** *master;* **adj:** *this;* **do:** *bird;* **s:** *we;* **hv:** *will;* **v:** *have;* **art:** *the;* **adj:** *greatest;* **do:** *hunter;* **prep:** *in;* **adj:** *all;* **op:** *Arabia;* **adv:** *perhaps;* **prep:** *in;* **adj:** *all;* **art:** *the;* **op:** *world;* **exp:** *There;* **lv:** *is;* **art:** *a;* **adj:** *long;* **s:** *road;* **pa:** *ahead;* **cc:** *but;* **s:** *we;* **hv:** *will;* **v:** *take;* **do:** *it;* **adv:** *together)*

3. Circle the superlative adjective. *(greatest)*
   Write its comparative and root forms: *(greater, great)*

4. Underline the parallel structure in the first sentence.
   (in all Arabia; in all the world)

5. Draw brackets around each clause. Mark any independent clauses with **ind** and any dependent clauses with **dep**. **(dep:** *[Ali, if we can master this bird];* **ind:** *[we will have the greatest hunter in all Arabia, perhaps in all the world];* **ind:** *[There is a long road ahead];* **ind:** *[but we will take it together])*

6. Based on your analysis, what is the structure of the first sentence?
   Simple   Compound   Complex   Compound-Complex

   What is the structure of the second?
   Simple   Compound   Complex   Compound-Complex

7. Write a homophone for **road**. *(rode, rowed)*

8. The word **master** is a homograph. We have given you one meaning; you write another.
   master verb: to overcome *(Sample answer:* **master** **noun:** *one who has control)*

9. Rewrite the first clause of the second sentence so that the subject comes before the verb. **(Sample answers:** *A long road lies ahead of us. –OR– We have a long road ahead of us.)*

10. Are Ali and the speaker going on a trip? No, the "long road" at the end of this passage is a
    simile   metaphor.
    What does the "long road" really describe? *(the amount of work required to train the eagle to be a hunter)*

11. Think of at least three words or phrases you could use instead of the phrase **long road** in the clause **There is a long road ahead**. **(Sample answers:** *difficult task, long process, huge project, arduous journey)*

Grammar 5: Sheet 65 Answer Guide

Passage

Ali and the Golden Eagle, p. 117:

Mom or Dad: Please review **ellipses**.

     ind   dep

[This village [that had lived

virtually unchanged for thousands

of years] was about to be hurtled

                       ind cc art

into the twentieth century]. [And a

adj   s   prep   op   prep

fourteen-year-old boy (from one) (of

art   adv   adj   op   prep   op

the most remote spots) (in Arabia)

hv   hv   v   prep art   adj

was being catapulted (into the mod-

      op

ern world)...all because of an eagle].

Exercises

1. Draw brackets around each clause. Mark any independent clauses with **ind** and any dependent clauses with **dep**. *(ind: [This village...was about to be hurtled into the twentieth century]; dep: [that had lived virtually unchanged for thousands of years]; ind: [And a fourteen-year-old boy from one of the most remote spots in Arabia was being catapulted into the modern world... all because of an eagle])*

    What is the structure of the first sentence?

    Simple Compound Complex Compound-Complex

    And what is the structure of the second?

    Simple Compound Complex Compound-Complex

2. Overall, what type of paragraph is this?

    Expository Persuasive Descriptive Narrative

3. What is the tense of the dependent clause in the first sentence?

    Simple Past Continuing Past Past Perfect

    What is the tense of the second sentence?

    Simple Past Continuing Past Past Perfect

4. Circle the ellipsis. What is its purpose here?

    To show a pause To show omitted words

5. Put arrows above the hyphens. *(fourteen-year-old)*

    What are they there for? (Check all that apply.)

    - [x] **To form an adjective**
    - [x] **To create a compound word**
    - [ ] **To show that something is missing**
    - [ ] **To avoid confusion or awkward spelling**
    - [x] **To create a new word**
    - [ ] **There is no good reason to include a hyphen**
    - [ ] **To create a number between twenty-one and ninety-nine**

6. Analyze the second sentence up to the ellipsis. *(cc: And; art: a; adj: fourteen-year-old; s: boy; prep: from; op: one; prep: of; art: the; adv: most; adj: remote; op: spots; prep: in; op: Arabia; hv: was; hv: being; v: catapulted; prep: into; art: the; adj: modern; op: world)*

7. The author wrote this paragraph in the passive voice. Please rewrite the entire paragraph in an active voice. *(**Sample answer:** This village had lived virtually unchanged for thousands of years and the eagle was about to hurtle it into the twentieth century. The eagle was about to catapult a fourteen-year-old boy from one of the most remote spots in Arabia into the modern world as well.)*

    Which version do you like better—the passive or active voice? **Passive Active**

    (Answers will vary—keep in mind that passive voice isn't always bad! The second sentence may even be easier to read in passive voice.)

Passage

King of the Wind, p. 35:

Mom or Dad: Please review **reflexive** and **intensive** **pronouns**.

Agba smothered a cry. Unmindful of <u>his</u> own safety, he thrust ⟨himself⟩

between Signor Achmet and the

part

foal. He fell to <u>his</u> knees, lifting the

tiny foal <u>whose</u> legs beat a tattoo in

the air. With a look of triumph, he

pointed to the white spot on the off

hind heel.

adj   *s*   *v*

<u>Signor Achmet's</u> eyes narrowed.

adj   *s*   *v*   *adv*   *prep* *art* *adj*

<u>His</u> brows came together (in a black

op   *part*

line). Agba could see him weighing

the two in <u>his</u> mind—the white spot

against the wheat ear. <u><u>The good</u></u>

art   *s*

<u><u>sign against the bad</u></u>. The scales

v   *adv*

tipped even.

Exercises

1. Underline the possessive nouns and pronouns. *(his [safety], his [knees], whose [legs], Signor Achmet's [eyes], His [brows], his [mind])*

2. Circle the reflexive pronoun. *(himself)*

3. Write **part** above the participles **lifting** and **weighing**, then draw arrows from them to the nouns or pronouns they modify. *(lifting-He; weighing-him)*

4. Rewrite the third sentence so that you replace the participle **lifting** with a verb. (***Sample answer:*** *He fell to his knees and lifted the tiny foal whose legs were beating a tattoo in the air.)*

5. Double underline the sentence fragment. Please rewrite it as a complete sentence. *(The good sign against the bad.* ***Sample answer:*** *Agba could see him weighing the good sign against the bad.)*

6. Analyze the first, second, and last sentences of the second paragraph. If you find a prepositional phrase, please surround it with parentheses. (**adj:** *Signor Achmet's;* **s:** *eyes;* **v:** *narrowed;* **adj:** *His;* **s:** *brows;* **v:** *came;* **adv:** *together;* **prep:** *in;* **art:** *a;* **adj:** *black;* **op:** *line;* **prep phrase:** *(in a black line);* **art:** *The;* **s:** *scales;* **v:** *tipped;* **adv:** *even)*

7. There is a punctuation error in the last sentence of the first paragraph. Please make the correction and circle it. *(there is a comma missing after the word* ***triumph)***

8. **Challenge:** What does it mean to **beat a tattoo**? *(to drum a military signal)*

Grammar 5: Sheet 67 Answer Guide

Passage

King of the Wind, p. 44:

Mom or Dad: Please review **italics**.

    ind   *dep*

[What did it matter] [if the other

                ind

colts thought] [Sham was different]?

ind   *ind*   s   v   prep adj   op

[He was]! [*They* ran (to their moth-

  dep/adv   s   lv   pa   cc prep

ers)] [when they were hungry or (in

  op   *ind*/cc   adj   s   lv   art

trouble)]. [But Sham's mother was a

  adj   adj   pn

slim brown horseboy].

Exercises

1. Draw brackets around each clause. Mark any independent clauses with **ind** and any dependent clauses with **dep**. *(***ind:*** [What did it matter]; **dep:** [if the other colts thought]; **ind:** [Sham was different]; **ind:** [He was]; **ind:** [They ran to their mothers]; **dep:** [when they were hungry or in trouble]; **ind:** [But Sham's mother was a slim brown horseboy])*

2. Indicate the structure for each sentence.

   First:

   Simple Compound Complex Compound-Complex

   Second:

   Simple Compound Complex Compound-Complex

   Third:

   Simple Compound Complex Compound-Complex

3. Evaluate the sentences indicated below, then circle the correct type for each:

   First:

   Imperative Interrogative Exclamatory Declarative

   Second:

   Imperative Interrogative Exclamatory Declarative

   Third:

   Imperative Interrogative Exclamatory Declarative

4. The first sentence asks a question but without expecting an answer. What is that called?

   An exhortative question   **A rhetorical question**

   An arboreal question   **An understood question**

5. Analyze the last two sentences. *(***s:*** They; **v:** ran; **prep:** to; **adj:** their; **op:** mothers; **adv:** when; **s:** they; **lv:** were; **pa:** hungry; **cc:** or; **prep:** in; **op:** trouble; **cc:** But; **adj:** Sham's; **s:** mother; **lv:** was; **art:** a; **adj:** slim; **adj:** brown; **pn:** horseboy)*

6. Why is **They** italicized?   **It is a title**   **For emphasis**

7. Please rewrite the second sentence to include all information a reader needs to know what Sham **was**. *(**Sample answer:** He was different from the other colts!)*

Grammar 5: Sheet 68 Answer Guide

Passage

King of the Wind, p. 122:

        nda   **n**   **nda**   **n**
"My poor boy! My poor boy!"

Mistress Cockburn said over and

                       n
over. Then she opened her hamper

           n   **n**
and placed a tart in Agba's hand.

 s   **v**   **io**   **art do/n prep**
She gave Grimalkin a crust (of

 adj   **op/n**   **cc** **adv**
Cheshire cheese cake) and quickly

    v   **art** **do/n**
covered the basket to hide the

                    n
brightly scrubbed carrots.

Exercises

1. Write **nda** above the nouns of direct address. *(My poor boy! My poor boy!)*

2. Circle the proper nouns and write **n** above the common nouns. There is one noun phrase composed of two nouns, one of which is used as an adjective. Include this phrase also. *(boy, boy, **Mistress Cockburn**, hamper, tart, **Agba**, hand, **Grimalkin**, crust, **Cheshire**, cheese cake, basket, carrots)*

3. Draw boxes around the possessive nouns and pronouns. *(My, My, her, Agba's)*

4. **Scrubbed** is a participle. Draw an arrow that points from it to the noun it modifies. *(scrubbed—carrots)*

5. What is the structure of the first sentence?
   Simple Compound Complex Compound-Complex
   What kind of predicate does it have?
   Simple Compound
      Mom or Dad: over and over is a compound adverb; there is only a single verb in this sentence.

6. What is the structure of the second sentence (the one that begins **Then she opened …**)?
   Simple Compound Complex Compound-Complex
   What kind of predicate does it have?
   Simple **Compound**

7. And the third sentence? What is its structure?
   Simple Compound Complex Compound-Complex
   What kind of predicate does it have?
   Simple **Compound**

8. Analyze the last sentence through the word **basket**. *(**s:** She; **v:** gave; **io:** Grimalkin; **art:** a; **do:** crust; **prep:** of; **adj:** Cheshire; **op:** cheese cake; **cc:** and; **adv:** quickly; **v:** covered; **art:** the; **do:** basket)*

9. Ms. Henry says Mistress Cockburn covered the basket **quickly**. Please think of and write at least three other adverbs or adverbial phrases or clauses Ms. Henry could have used to describe the manner in which Mistress Cockburn covered the basket. Make sure you include at least one phrase or clause. (Remember: prepositional phrases can serve as adverbs!) *(**Sample answers:** with a bang; with work-worn hands; slowly; deftly; without a sound)*

Grammar 5: Sheet 69 Answer Guide

Passage

Louis Braille, p. 15:

Mom or Dad: Please read the note under question #9 before you begin today.

     s   lv   pa   adv
People sounded different too.

adj   s   v art adj   do
One man had a deep cough.

   s   v   art do   prep   op
Another had the habit (of whistling)

   prep   adj   op
(through his teeth). A third man

      prep   op
walked (with a limp). "Don't you

         prep   op
see?" Louis felt (like saying). "There

are so many ways to tell people

apart—if only you listen!"

Exercises

1. Write **prep** above all prepositions, **op** above all objects of prepositions, and draw parentheses around all prepositional phrases. **Hint:** The word **like** in the next-to-last sentence is a preposition. *(of **whistling**; through his **teeth**; with a **limp**; like **saying**)*

2. Since **like** is a preposition, what is the word **saying**?

   A verb   A participle   A gerund   An infinitive

   Mom or Dad: Notice that when we say we feel like ____, the blank is always a noun. So when we say we feel like **doing** something or **saying** something, the words **doing** and **saying** are gerunds, and the things we want to do or say are, properly, the objects of the gerunds.

3. Underline the interrogative sentence. *(Don't you see?)*

4. What type of sentence is the last one?

   Imperative Interrogative Exclamatory Declarative

5. Analyze the first through third sentences. **(s:** *People;* **lv:** *sounded;* **pa:** *different;* **adv:** *too;* **adj:** *One;* **s:** *man;*

v: *had;* **art:** *a;* **adj:** *deep;* **do:** *cough;* **s:** *Another;* **v:** *had;* **art:** *the;* **do:** *habit;* **prep:** *of;* **op:** *whistling;* **prep:** *through;* **adj:** *his;* **op:** *teeth)*

6. What is the tense of the last sentence?

   Past Present Future

7. What is the person (first, second, or third) of Louis' quote? **First Second Third**

8. Rewrite the third sentence to eliminate the gerund **whistling**. *(**Sample answers:** Another whistled through his teeth. It was his habit. –OR– Another habitually whistled through his teeth.)*

9. Discuss with Mom or Dad: Is the first sentence a good topic sentence?

   ☐ **Yes**
   ☐ **No**
   ☐ **Another would be better**
   ☐ **There really isn't a good topic sentence in the paragraph**

   Why?

   Mom or Dad: We've included this question primarily so you and your child can talk about it.

   The truth is, we're torn on this one. The first sentence certainly summarizes what the next two sentences are about and it could also summarize what the third sentence tells us. (However, the third following sentence doesn't specifically mention a sound; we have to infer that a man who walks with a limp will sound differently than other people who don't.)

   But the first sentence in no way summarizes the meaning contained in the last two sentences of the paragraph. So on that ground, we would say the first sentence does *not* make a good topic sentence. Indeed, we would say there is probably no good topic sentence for the paragraph as a whole.

   However... (Teaching opportunity!)

   If we were to make two relatively minor adjustments to the paragraph, we could eventually arrive at a very fine topic sentence. Consider:

   > "There are so many ways to tell people apart—if only you listen!" Louis felt like saying. People sounded different. One man had a deep cough. Another had the habit of whistling through his teeth. A third man walked with a limp.

10. Circle the homophones of: **two, won, threw, sea, their, sew, weighs, yew.** *(too, One, through, see, There, so, ways, you)*

Grammar 5: Sheet 70 Answer Guide

Passage

Star of Light, p. 93:

Mom or Dad: Please review **sentence fragments** and **attributions**.

       s   v   art adj   do   adv

Hamid faced the little boy shyly.

s v   prep adj   op   s   v

"I'm (from the country)," he said.

"Why have you come to town?"

asked the boy.

     frag

"To find work."

"Where are your mother and

father?"

     frag

"Dead."

"Where do you live?"

     frag

"In the street."

Exercises

1. Write **frag** above the sentence fragments. (**frag:** *"To find work."* **frag:** *"Dead."* **frag:** *"In the street."*)

2. Rewrite the sentence fragments as complete sentences. (**Sample answers:** *"I have come to town in order to find work." "My mother and father are dead." "I live in the street."*)

3. Do you think the book would be better if these fragments were written as complete sentences? **Yes** **No** *(Since it is dialog, we don't think it would be better at all; it would sound horribly stuffy and stilted! Normal people just don't talk that way! We use sentence fragments when we speak.)*

4. In the space available beside each unattributed quotation, please write an attribution. You may place the attribution either before or after the quotation. If you need to change a period to a comma, do so. See if you can provide enough variety in your attributions so that the dialog will feel fresh and vibrant. (**Sample answers:** *Hamid replied: "To find work." –OR– "To find work," Hamid replied. // The boy persisted: "Where are your mother and father?" –OR– "Where are your mother and father?" the boy probed. // "Dead," said Hamid dully. –OR– Hamid sighed heavily as he remembered. "Dead," he replied. // And then the boy asked the natural question: "Where do you live?" –OR– "Where do you live?" the boy asked finally. // Hamid's voice took on a hard edge as he said, "In the street." –OR– "In the street," Hamid answered, and his voice had the hard edge of one who is not sure whether to trust his inquisitor or to fight.*)

Once you have written all your attributions: do you think the passage is better for the attributions?

Yes No

(Answers will vary.)

    Mom or Dad: Please discuss this question and answer with your child. Think it through together.

5. Hamid, we are told, **faced the little boy shyly**. Please think of at least four other adverbs you could use to describe how Hamid could have faced the little boy. Make sure you include at least one prepositional phrase. (**Sample answers:** *boldly; with fierce determination; with a smile; in the manner of one who begs alms; with a wary eye; bitterly*)

6. What does it mean to live **in the street**? *(not in a building, in a shelter, on the street)*

7. Analyze the first two sentences. (**s:** *Hamid;* **v:** *faced;* **art:** *the;* **adj:** *little;* **do:** *boy;* **adv:** *shyly;* **s:** *I;* **v:** *[a]m;* **prep:** *from;* **art:** *the;* **op:** *country;* **s:** *he;* **v:** *said*)

Grammar 5: Sheet 71 Answer Guide

Passage

Star of Light, p. 123:

Mom or Dad: Please review **coordinating conjunctions** and **capitalization of titles**.

<pre>
  s lv art   pn/✓ prep art   op/✓
"It's the Feast (of the Christians)
  adv   v   art   n/s   prep art
today," explained the nurse (to the
     adj   adj   op/n   cc s   v
wide-eyed little boys), "so I thought
  s   hv   v   do   adv
we would keep it together. It is the
    ✓   prep   op/n   prep   op/✓
Feast (of the birth) (of Jesus Christ).
                        n   ✓
He was the greatest gift God ever
       cc prep   op/✓
gave, so (at His Feast) we all give
    n   prep   op
presents (to each other). That is why
  ✓   n   cc
Kinza has a rubber ball, and that
                              n   cc
is why I've bought you sweets and
  n   cc   n
oranges and bananas."
</pre>

Exercises

1. Write **n** above the common nouns and place check marks above the proper nouns. Do not count as nouns those nouns that are being used as adjectives. *(**Feast**; **Christians**; nurse; boys; **Feast**; birth; **Jesus Christ**; gift; **God**; **Feast** [or, **His Feast**]; presents; **Kinza**; ball; sweets; oranges; bananas)*

   Mom or Dad: If your child marked the entire phrase **Feast of the birth of Jesus Christ** as a proper noun, we would not count it wrong. See question #9.

2. Write **prep** above all prepositions, **op** above all objects of prepositions, and draw parentheses around all prepositional phrases. *(of the **Christians**; to the wide-eyed*

little **boys**; of the **birth**; of **Jesus Christ**; at His **Feast**; to each **other**)

3. Please copy the contractions in the spaces below, then write the original words for which they stand. *(It's–It is; I've–I have)*

4. Underline the parallel phrases in the passage. *(That is why Kinza...That is why I've...)*

5. Draw an arrow that points to the hyphen. Why is it there? (Check all that apply.)
   - [x] **To form an adjective**
   - [x] **To create a compound word**
   - [ ] **To show that something is missing**
   - [ ] **To avoid confusion or awkward spelling**
   - [ ] **To create a new word**
   - [ ] **There is no good reason to include a hyphen**
   - [ ] **To create a number between twenty-one and ninety-nine**

6. Please list the seven coordinating conjunctions. *(FANBOYS: for, and, not, but, or, yet, so)* Use **cc** to label them in the passage. *(so, so, and, and, and)*

7. Analyze the first sentence. *(**s:** It; **lv:** [i]'s; **art:** the; **pn:** Feast; **prep:** of; **art:** the; **op:** Christians; **adv:** today; **v:** explained; **art:** the; **s:** nurse; **prep:** to; **art:** the; **adj:** wide-eyed; **adj:** little; **op:** boys; **cc:** so; **s:** I; **v:** thought; **s:** we; **hv:** would; **v:** keep; **do:** it; **adv:** together)*

8. Suppose the entire phrase **Feast of the birth of Jesus Christ** was considered the name or title of the feast. How would you write the phrase? In other words, what words would you capitalize? Write them here: *(Feast of the Birth of Jesus Christ)*

9. What is the common name for the **Feast of the birth of Jesus Christ**? *(Christmas)* Why do you think the lady doesn't use that word? *(**Sample answers:** 1) because the word has no meaning in this North African culture; 2) if it does have any meaning, it is likely to be the "wrong" meaning—i.e., referencing the standard secular view of the occasion; 3) the lady wants to get to the root issue—the birth of Jesus Christ—and not have to discuss the broader (secular) implications of the celebration)*

Grammar 5: Sheet 72 Answer Guide

Passage

Star of Light, pp. 161–162:

Mom or Dad: Please review **semicolons**.

"How does the light get into the empty lantern?" asked Rosemary.

"It's just a matter of opening a door and placing a candle inside. Jesus

   lv **art** **pn**   **cc**   **s** **v**   **inf**

is the Light, and He wants to come

adv **cc** **s**   **prep**   **op**   **v**   **art**

in; and we, (by believing), open the

  do   **cc**   **v**   **do** **adv**

door and ask Him in. Then, if the glass of the lantern is clean, the light shines out clearly; but if the glass is clouded and dirty the light will be very dim."

Exercises

1. Why do we find semicolons in the middle of the third and fourth sentences? (Check all that apply.)

    ☐ **To help join two independent clauses in one sentence—especially when they are long or contain commas**

    ☐ **To separate groups that contain commas**

    ☒ **To serve the kind of function that a period does when a comma would do; to provide a more substantial break than a comma would**

    ☐ **It shouldn't be there; the author should have used _____ instead**

    Mom or Dad: You may want to discuss how and why a comma can fulfill the same function as the semicolon when it helps to join two independent clauses.

2. What is the structure of the first sentence (including the attribution)?

    Simple Compound Complex Compound-Complex

    What is the structure of the second?

    Simple Compound Complex Compound-Complex

    What is the structure of the third?

    Simple **Compound** Complex Compound-Complex

    What is the structure of the fourth?

    Simple Compound Complex **Compound-Complex**

3. What are the tenses of the following clauses? If the glass is clouded and dirty…

    Past **Present** Future

    …the light will be very dim…

    Past Present **Future**

4. Double underline the interrogative sentence. *(How does the light get into the empty lantern?)*

5. Circle the antecedent to the pronoun **It** in the second sentence. *(How does the light get into the empty lantern? —the entire question)*

6. Think of two antonyms or, at least, contrastive expressions for each of the following words. Feel free to use prepositional phrases, clauses, or other longer means of expressing the opposite idea! (***Sample answers:*** **empty** *full, overflowing;* **open** *shut, close;* **light** *dark/ darkness/darken, murk/murky/murkiness;* **Aunt** *Uncle, cousin, niece, nephew;* **inside** *outside, round about, away from;* **him** *her, it;* **clearly** *dimly, darkly, murkily;* **clean** *dirty, messy, filthy)*

7. The last sentence includes a strong example of parallelism. Please underline the parallels and draw two-headed arrows that connect the parallel phrases. *(if the glass—if the glass; the light—the light)*

8. Analyze the third sentence. *(**s:** Jesus; **lv:** is; **art:** the; **pn:** Light; **cc:** and; **s:** He; **v:** wants; **inf:** to come; **adv:** in; **cc:** and; **s:** we; **prep:** by; **op:** believing; **v:** open; **art:** the; **do:** door; **cc:** and; **v:** ask; **do:** Him; **adv:** in)*

9. Rewrite the second sentence in such a way that you eliminate the gerunds **opening** and **placing**. (***Sample answer:*** *You need to open a door and place a candle inside.)*

Section Three
Resources

This page intentionally left blank.

List of Standard Symbols

Standard Abbreviations

adj—adjective

adj clause—adjectival clause

adv—adverb

adv clause—adverbial clause

ant—antecedent

appos—appositive

appos phrase—appositive phrase

art—article

cc—coordinating conjunction

conj—conjunction/conjunctive

corc—correlative conjunction

dem pro—demonstrative pronoun

dep—dependent clause

do—direct object

exp—expletive

ger—gerund

hv—helping verb

ind—independent clause

indef pro—indefinite pronoun

inf—infinitive

int—intransitive

inter pro—interrogative pronoun

interj—interjection

io—indirect object

lv—linking verb

n—noun

nda—noun of direct address

obj—object (used with verbals—gerunds, participles, and infinitives)

oc—object complement

op—object of the preposition

prep—preposition

prep phrase—prepositional phrase

part—participle

part phrase—participial phrase

pa—predicate adjective

pn—predicate noun

pro—pronoun

rel pro—relative pronoun

s—subject

sc—subordinating conjunction

trans—transitive

v—verb

Principal Parts

n—noun

pro—pronoun

indef pro—indefinite pronoun

inter pro—interrogative pronoun

rel pro—relative pronoun

ant—antecedent

appos—appositive

appos phrase—appositive phrase

s—subject

do—direct object

io—indirect object

nda—noun of direct address

exp—expletive

interj—interjection

v—verb

hv—helping verb

lv—linking verb

adj—adjective

adj clause—adjectival clause

adv—adverb

adv clause—adverbial clause

dem pro—demonstrative pronoun

obj—object (used with verbals—gerunds, participles, and infinitives)

oc—object complement

art—article

cc—coordinating conjunction

conj—conjunction/conjunctive

corc—correlative conjunction

sc—subordinating conjunction

dep—dependent clause

ind—independent clause

prep—preposition

op—object of the preposition

prep phrase—prepositional phrase

ger—gerund

inf—infinitive

part—participle

part phrase—participial phrase

pa—predicate adjective

pn—predicate noun ■

This page intentionally left blank.

Grammar Guide

Abbreviations

Abbreviations are shortened versions of commonly used words.

Ex. Mr. (for Mister)
St. (for Street or Saint)

TELL ME MORE!

One of the most common abbreviations is *Mr.* to stand for *Mister* and *Mrs.* which stands for *Missus* which, in itself, is a shortened version of *Mistress*. Normally, you indicate that you are using an abbreviation by putting a period after the abbreviation. Some more examples: *Dr.* for *Drive* or *Doctor*; *Blvd.* for *Boulevard*; *etc.* for *etcetera*.

An **acronym** is a special kind of abbreviation that does not need a period and is pronounced as one word.

Ex. NASA (National Aeronautics and Space Administration)

An **initialism** is a special kind of abbreviation in which each letter used to form the abbreviation is pronounced separately. Like acronyms, initialisms do not need periods.

Ex. FBI (Federal Bureau of Investigation)

Acronym (see Abbreviations)

Action Verb (see Verb)

Active Voice (see Voice)

Adjective

An **adjective** describes or modifies a noun.

Ex. *Green* book
Sleepy girl
Hot potato

TELL ME MORE!

*Adj*ectives *add* to our understanding of nouns. If you have a box (noun), and then say it is soft, hot, dark, and wet, the words *soft, hot, dark,* and *wet* are all **adjectives**. If you are talking about a young man, *young* is an adjective; it describes the man. In yellow flower, *yellow* is an adjective; it describes the flower. If you are talking about his satin shirt, *his* and *satin* both serve as adjectives that describe the shirt.

Notice that some words—like *soft, hot,* and *dark*— are always and only adjectives. Other words—like *satin* and *his*—can serve as adjectives but are nouns (*satin*) and pro-

nouns (*his*) as well. Notice, too, that even verbs can serve as adjectives: the *shining* star, a *crumpled* sheet of paper.

You can string adjectives together.

Ex. The *green* men ate. The *three green* men ate.
The *three tall green* men ate.
The *three strong tall green* men ate.

Adjectives come in one of three forms: positive, comparative, or superlative. The **positive form** modifies a word without comparing it to anything else. For example: That dog is big. The **comparative form** modifies a word by comparing it to one other thing. Comparative adjectives often use the ending -er or the words *more* or *less*. For example: That dog is bigger than my dog. The **superlative form** modifies a word by comparing it to two or more other things. Superlative adjectives often use the ending -est or the words most or least.

Ex.: That dog is the biggest dog on my block.

For further information about special types of adjectives, see *Article, Determiner,* and *Quantifier.*

Adjective/Adjectival Clause (see Clause)

Adverb

An adverb adds to or modifies our understanding of a verb. Adverbs tell us how, when, or where the verb happened (or is happening or will yet happen). They can also describe or modify our under-standing of an adjective or another adverb.

Ex: The green men ate *quickly*. (*Quickly* describes how the verb ate.)

The woman walked *slowly*. (*Slowly* describes the verb walked.)

Josh fell *down*. (*Down* is an adverb because it describes the verb fall. It tells us about Josh's falling: He fell *down*)

Emily will feel better *tomorrow*. (*Tomorrow* describes when Emily will feel better.)

The *deep* green moss grew. (*Deep* describes the adjective green.)

The green moss grew *extremely quickly*. (*Quickly* describes how the moss grew. *Extremely* describes the other adverb, *quickly*.)

TELL ME MORE!

Here's a clue that will help you identify many adverbs: if you find a word that ends in -*ly*, it is almost assuredly an adverb.

In the phrase *talk loudly*, the verb *talk* is modified by the adverb *loudly*. How did he talk? He talked loudly. Loudly adds to our understanding of talk. How about the phrase *worked hard*? Which word is the verb that tells us what happened? (*worked* is the verb) And which is the adverb that tells us how the person or machine worked? (*hard* is the adverb) How about *suddenly remembered*? What is the verb and what is the adverb? (*remembered* is the verb; *suddenly* is the adverb)

You can find adverbs right next to the verbs they modify—either in front of or after the verb; and you can find them at distances from their verbs.

> Ex. He *quickly* jumped on the horse.
>
> He jumped *quickly* onto the horse.
>
> *Quickly*, the large man jumped onto the horse.
>
> He jumped onto the galloping horse *quickly*—before it got away.

Examples of adverbs that modify adjectives: in the phrase *the very bright light*, *very* is an adverb; it modifies the adjective *bright*. (Notice that very does not modify *light*! You can't have a very light!) In *tremendously loud engine*, *tremendously* is an adverb; it modifies the adjective *loud*; you can have a *loud* engine and a *tremendously loud* engine, but you can't have a *tremendously* engine.

Adverbs come in one of three forms: positive, comparative, or superlative. The **positive form** modifies a word without comparing it to anything else. For example: He runs fast. The **comparative form** modifies a word by comparing it to one other thing. Comparative adverbs often use the ending *-er* or the words *more* or *less*. For example: He runs faster than my dog. The **superlative form** modifies a word by comparing it to two or more other things. Superlative adverbs often use the ending *-est* or the words *most* or *least*. For example: He runs the fastest of all the dogs on my block.

Adverbs add power to your writing. Use them often.

Adverb/Adverbial Clause (see Clause)

Agreement (see Subject-Verb Agreement)

Alphabetization

Alphabetization is the process of placing a series of words in alphabetical order—in order from a to z beginning with the first letter of the word. When two words start with the same letter, then you compare their second letters. When two words share the same first and second letters, then you compare the third letters . . . and so on until you find a letter on which they disagree.

> Ex. aardvark, adjective, adverb, amber, ambulance

Analogy

An analogy compares two (or more) things that, although otherwise dissimilar, are similar in some important way. Analogies are used to suggest that because two (or more) things are similar in some way they are also similar in some further way. For further information about special types of analogies, see *Simile* and *Metaphor*.

> Ex. Phil hates receiving unsolicited "spam" e-mail because deleting it from his inbox wastes so much time. He insists there must be some solution to this problem on the horizon! Of course, he also used to think that, by now, he wouldn't need to continually pitch the "junk" mail that accumulates in his mailbox on a daily basis. (The analogy in this paragraph suggests that "spam" e-mail, like postal "junk" mail, may be here to stay!)

Antecedent

An antecedent is the noun that a pronoun refers to.

> Ex. *Emily* cooked breakfast. She is a good cook. (*Emily* is the antecedent for the pronoun *she*.)

TELL ME MORE!
"*Ante*" means "before" or "in front of." The noun to which the pronoun refers usually comes before or "*ante*" the pronoun.

When you say, He came, the person you're talking to wants to know "Who is he? To whom are you referring when you talk about him or he?" If you answer, "Oh! I'm talking about John (or whoever)," John (or whoever) is the **antecedent**. That is the noun to which he refers.

Antecedents are extremely important, especially when you begin to use pronouns. For example, read the following sentences: Mike and Tim were talking. Tim said he could marry Sarah because he didn't mind if Sarah didn't like him. Every pronoun in the second sentence must have an antecedent or an implied antecedent. Tim is obviously the one who's talking. Tim says he (who? Tim? Mike? Someone else?) could marry Sarah because he (who?) didn't mind if Sarah didn't like him (again, who is Tim talking about?). Never use a pronoun unless you know that its antecedent is obvious! Besides the pronouns where it is very obvious that you need to know the antecedent, there are a few pronouns where you can usually figure out what the antecedent is . . . even if no one tells you.

> Ex. I/me/my
> you/your/yours
> we/us/our/ours

Antonym

An antonym is a word that means the opposite of another word.

> Ex. *Up* is the opposite of—or antonym for—*down*
> *Cold* is the antonym for *hot*
> *Out* is the antonym for *in*.

Apostrophe

An apostrophe (') is a punctuation mark that can show possession, make contractions, or show when letters are left out. Apostrophes are also used to make letters, numbers, and signs plural.

> Ex. the kids' cookbook (the cookbook belongs to the kids)
>
> didn't (did not)
>
> I'm waitin' for him. (shortened version of *waiting*)
>
> Z's, 9's, $'s

Appositive

An appositive is a noun or noun phrase (**appositive phrase**) that renames or describes the nouns or pronouns that come immediately before it. Appositives are usually surrounded—or set off by—commas.

> Ex. Mark, *first baseman for the Rangers*, had a strong season.
>
> Carmen, *a mother of three*, barely had time to make dinner.
>
> My guitar, *an Ibanez*, is a real beauty.

TELL ME MORE!

Use an appositive when you want to say something important about the subject, but you want the sentence itself to focus on something you consider even more important. So, for example, you want to say that *Samson lost all his strength when he cut his hair*. That is the main message you want to tell people. But in order for them to really understand what you are saying, you need to tell them that he was normally a strong man. So you insert the appositive: Samson, *a strong man*, lost all his strength when he cut his hair.

Appositive Phrase (see Appositive)

Article

An article is a special type of adjective. There are three articles—*the*, *a*, and *an*. Articles tell something about the nouns that follow them.

> Ex. *The* dogs fight
> *A* plane flies
> *An* apple falls.

TELL ME MORE!

The is called a **definite article**, because it defines exactly which one: the specific apple that we've been talking about or the apple that we are about to talk about. *The* tells you that the noun that follows is a particular one.

> Ex. *The* apple (one specific apple)
> *An* apple (any apple)

A and *An* are called **indefinite articles**, because you can't be sure which particular item they are talking about. They just say that it is some item. *A* and *an* mean the same thing. *A* is used when the noun that follows it begins with a consonant sound. *An* is used when the noun that follows it begins with a vowel sound.

> Ex. *a* boa constrictor
> *a* one-dollar bill
> *an* ant
> *an* hour

Attribution

An attribution is the phrase that indicates who said whatever is being quoted.

> Ex. Eddie said
> Josh yelled
> Caitlyn laughed

TELL ME MORE!

An attribution can be placed before, in the middle of, or after the quotation. When the attribution is before the quotation, identify who is being quoted, follow that with a comma, and then begin the quotation.

> Ex. *Michael said*, "I sure am hungry."
> *Duane says*, "I love to eat Italian food."

When an attribution is in the middle of a quotation, attach the attribution to whatever comes before it. Then, follow the attribution with a comma and treat it and the quotation that follows as if the attribution were before the quotation.

> Ex. "I love that idea!" *said Amber*. "This will be so much fun."
>
> "I'm not sure," *commented Chase*, "if it will work."

When an attribution is placed at the end of the quotation and the quotation ends with a period, replace the period with a comma and follow the comma with the closing quotation mark. Then, write the attribution.

Ex. "We can figure this out," *Pam said.*

"I'm happy with whatever everybody else wants," *Kelly stated.*

However, when a quotation ends with an exclamation point or a question mark, those punctuation marks must be retained. Don't replace them with commas.

Ex. "Can I hang out with you guys?" *Bo asks.*
"Yes you can!" *Sondra answers.*

In dialog, you should always begin a new paragraph whenever a new speaker begins to talk. You should never have two or more speakers speak one after the other in a single paragraph. It is not always necessary to attribute each statement in dialog. If two people are conversing, once you have told your audience who the two speakers are, and once they begin talking back and forth, the change of paragraph alone can serve to indicate that the speakers have changed.

Ex. "Sam the ram can pass Val the nag," said Matt.
"Oh, sure!" said Jen.
"He can! He can! I'll prove it to you."
"Oh, yeah? How?"

Many authors attribute quotations with the simple word *said*. There is nothing wrong with using said. When writing dialog, you want people to focus on the words that the characters are saying rather than—or, at least, more than—they focus on the attributions. But! Sometimes it is helpful to use interesting words. If you use said in every paragraph, readers can become bored.

Ex. Joe Felder *asked*, "What are you doing?"
Julian *replied*, "Nothing."

Auxiliary Verb (see Helping Verb)

Being Verb (see Verb)

Brackets

Brackets ([ ]) are marks of punctuation used within quoted material to set off additional and/or clarifying information or to indicate editorial corrections.

Ex. "She [the author's wife] is my greatest source of support."

"I'd like to buy twenty-seven [baseballs] before the start of the season."

Brackets may also be substituted for parentheses within parentheses for added clarity.

Ex. The fish tank (which is 39 gallons [the largest the store carries, of course] and very large) needs to be cleaned soon.

Capitalization

Capitalization is the process of capitalizing—beginning words with upper-case letters. You should always capitalize all proper nouns, titles, and the first word in a sentence.

Ex. Some people believe that George Washington, the first President of the United States, could not tell a lie.

TELL ME MORE!

There are many specific rules regarding capitalization, a few more of which are summarized below.

Ex. Sections of the country (Northwest) (But don't capitalize words merely indicating direction: Drive north two miles, and then go four more miles east.)

Religions, races, languages, and nationalities (Christian, English, Japanese)

References to God, the Bible, and books of the Bible (the Lord, the Word, Exodus)

Titles (Denver Post, Discipleship Journal)

Associations, teams, or organizations (Colorado Avalanche, Republican Party)

Abbreviations (CIA, FBI, NASA)

Letters used to indicate shape or form (U-turn, T-shirt)

Words used as or part of proper names (Uncle Randy, Dad) (But don't capitalize such words if they are not being used to replace or complement proper nouns: Ask your mom for some money.)

Titles of courses (Psychology 101) (But don't capitalize such words when used to refer to a field of study: I am a psychology major.)

Days, months, and holidays (Monday, January, Easter)

Special events or periods of history (the Boston Tea Party, the Dark Ages)

Trade names (Nissan Xterra, Rio Karma)

Geographical references (Earth, North America, Indonesia, Colorado, Indianapolis, Broadway, Southwest, San Juan Mountains, Ohio River, Washington Square Park) (But don't capitalize general geographic references: We love to swim in the ocean.)

Clause

A clause is a group of related words that includes a subject and a predicate. All complete sentences include at least one clause. Many sentences include two or more clauses.

Ex. Will (*subject*) slept (*predicate*). Pete (*subject*) ate ice cream all night (*predicate*) [*clause*]; then he (*subject*) felt sick the next day (*predicate*) [*clause*].

TELL ME MORE!

Some clauses have one subject but two or more predicates:

Ex. Stan (*subject*) walked (*predicate*) and jumped (*predicate*).

The actress (*subject*) stumbled (*predicate*) at the top of the stairs, almost recovered (*predicate*), but fell (*predicate*) anyway.

Some clauses have two or more subjects to whom or to which the same predicates apply:

Ex. The bobcat (*subject*) and coyote (*subject*) howled (*predicate*) and screeched (*predicate*).

Sarah (*subject*), Jenny (*subject*), and Lisa (*subject*) crashed (*predicate*) into each other at the top of the stairs, stumbled (*predicate*) a moment, almost recovered (*predicate*), but fell (*predicate*) anyway.

If different predicates apply to different subjects, then you have separate clauses.

Ex. Stan (*subject*) stayed up all night (*predicate*) [*clause*]; then he (*subject*) slept the next day (*predicate*) [*clause*].

The bobcat (*subject*) howled (*predicate*) [*clause*] while the coyote (*subject*) screeched (*predicate*) [*clause*].

Sarah (*subject*), Jenny (*subject*), and Lisa (*subject*) crashed into each other at the top of the stairs (*predicate*) [*clause*], but it was Michael (*subject*) and Barry (*subject*) who fell (*predicate*) [*clause*].

Clauses can serve different functions within a sentence. **Adjective** (or **adjectival** or **relative**) **clauses** usually begin with a relative pronoun and serve as an adjective.

Ex. That tumbled to the floor

Whose blond hair shimmered in the light

Adverb (or **adverbial**) **clauses** usually begin with a subordinating conjunction and serve as an adverb.

Ex. When the clock strikes twelve

Where the stream meets the river

See *Relative Pronoun* or *Subordinating Conjunction* for more information.

Cleft Sentence

A cleft sentence is a complex sentence formed when an original declarative sentence is divided ("cleft") into two clauses—a main clause and a subordinate clause—for the purpose of emphasizing a particular part of the sentence. Cleft sentences usually begin with either the word *there* or *it*, followed by some form of the verb *to be*.

Ex. Original sentence: Michael came up with the idea for the new lunch plan.

Cleft sentence: It was Michael who came up with the idea for the new lunch plan.

TELL ME MORE!

Cleft sentences have delayed subjects. In other words, the true subject of a cleft sentence is not *there* or *it*; the true subject—if there is one—is whatever noun follows the verb. See also *Subject*.

If *there* and *it* are not subjects, what are they? They are called expletives, because they simply fulfill a structural function within the sentence. See also *Expletive*.

Cleft sentences can also be created with *what*. Cleft sentences beginning with *what* will usually make an initial noun clause out of the primary verb of the sentence:

Ex. Your stubborn attitude caused this problem.

What caused this problem is your stubborn attitude.

Colon

The colon (:) is a punctuation mark with many functions. Using a colon is like saying, "I'm going to tell you something important: Now here it is." What follows the colon usually explains or expands upon what came before. We use also use colons to introduce clauses, quotations, and lists.

Ex. Emphasis: He knew what frightened him: sky diving.

Quotations: A whisper floated in the air: "Help me!"

Lists: Sarah has plenty of toys: dolls, a playhouse, and a rocking horse.

Salutations: Dear President Bush: Time: 9:23pm

Chapter/Verse: Psalm 46:1 (also used to separate titles/subtitles and volumes/pages)

TELL ME MORE!

Colons should not come between verbs and their objects.

Ex. I have: a dog, a horse, and a rhinoceros. (incorrect)

I have several animals: a dog, a horse, and a rhinoceros. (correct)

Comma

The comma (,) is a versatile mark of punctuation. Among its many uses, one of the most prominent is as a separator, helping to add clarity to a sentence.

Ex. 1. Between independent clauses that are joined by a coordinating conjunction. (I went to the grocery store, but my best friend went to the hockey game.)

2. To separate items in a series. (I went to the grocery store to buy apples, soda, dog food, and laundry detergent.)

3. To separate nonrestrictive clauses from the rest of the sentence. (The grocery store, which was built last year, is always busy on Saturdays.)

4. To separate multiple adjectives. (It was an exciting, busy day at the grocery store.)

5. After introductory phrases or clauses. (After a hard day of work, I like to go grocery shopping.)

6. To set off dates or items in addresses. (On July 2, 1997, I went to the grocery store located at 7 Lucky Drive, Anytown, Colorado 54321.)

7. To clarify large numbers. (1,000 apples or 1,000,000 oranges)

8. To separate contrasted or parenthetical information. (Sue, not Judy, is the guilty one.)

9. To set off explanatory phrases or appositives. (Samson, my Weimaraner puppy, is fond of perpetual motion.)

10. To set off dialogue and nouns of direct address. ("Thad, put the spatula in the dishwasher," said Joan.)

11. To set off interjections or interruptions. (Hey, stop that! In my opinion, well, you just shouldn't be doing that.)

12. To set off titles or initials. (John F. Kennedy, Jr., started George magazine.)

13. To clarify otherwise confusing text. (What the production department does, does change the shipping department's work schedule.)

TELL ME MORE!

The series comma: always separate three or more items in a list by using *commas* between them. However, do not use commas between the members of a series composed of only two items—unless the comma is necessary for clarity's sake! If the last item in a list is preceded by the word *and*, you may, but you don't have to, place a comma between the next-to-last item in the list and the word *and*:

Ex. Please buy peanut butter, jelly, bread, graham crackers, and milk.

Please buy peanut butter, jelly, bread, graham crackers and milk.

Common Noun

A common noun is a general word that refers to a person, place, thing, or idea not named directly.

Ex.	Proper Noun	Common Noun
	Winston Churchill	man
	Maggie	girl
	Denver	city

Complements

A complement completes—or "complements"—the predicate in a sentence. A complement is an adjective, a noun, a phrase or clause that acts as an adjective or a noun.

Tell Me More

There are three types of complements:

Subject complements are predicate nouns and predicate adjectives. They follow a linking verb and modify or describe the subject:

Ex. Jason is my big *brother*.
Labradors are both *friendly* and *loyal*.

Object complements follow a direct object and modify or refer to the direct object:

Ex. Shannon painted her room *green*.
Mama named the baby *Brandon*.

Verb complements are the direct or indirect objects of a verb.

Ex.
    s   v   io   do
Bubba tossed *Brian* the *keys*.
    s   v   io   do
Idai wrote *Katie* a *note*.

Complete Predicate

The complete predicate is everything in a clause other than the complete subject, i.e., the simple or compound predicate plus all its modifiers.

Ex. Sondra's favorite restaurant *burned to the ground*. (*burned to the ground* is the complete predicate)

Complete Subject

The complete subject includes a simple or compound subject, as well as any words that modify or describe the subject—including adjectives, adverbs, and articles.

Ex. *Sondra's favorite restaurant* burned to the ground. (*restaurant* is the simple subject—*Sondra's favorite restaurant* is the complete subject)

Complex Sentence

A complex sentence consists of an independent clause and a dependent clause.

Ex. After a hard day of work (dependent clause), I like to go grocery shopping (independent clause).

When Phil saw April 1 on his calendar (dependent clause), he broke into a cold sweat (independent clause).

Compound Predicate

A compound predicate is made up of two or more simple predicates applied to a single subject. The subject and the compound predicate, together, still form one clause.

Ex. Sondra's favorite restaurant *caught on fire* and *burned to the ground.* (The simple predicates *caught on fire* and *burned to the ground* tell what happened to the single subject *restaurant.*)

The dog with only three legs *jumped through the ring of fire* and *rolled onto his side.* (The simple predicates *jumped through the ring of fire* and *rolled onto his side* describe what the single subject *dog* did.)

Compound Sentence

A compound sentence is composed of two or more simple sentences (independent clauses) that have been joined together in one of several ways.

Ex. By a coordinating conjunction (Pam saw the shark *and* she screamed.)

By a coordinating conjunction and a comma (I heard Pam's scream, *but* I could not see what had frightened her.)

By a semicolon (Pam screamed; Amber screamed; everyone ran!)

By a semicolon and a conjunctive adverb (I saw the shark; *however*, it didn't scare me.)

Compound Subject

A compound subject is made up of two or more simple subjects. The compound subject and its predicate(s), together, still form one clause.

Ex. *Ryan* and *Bo* love Japanese food.
Michael, Duane, and *Kelly* prefer Italian food.

Compound Word

A compound word is a word made up of two or more smaller words.

Ex. *campground* (camp/ground); *pillbox* (pill/box)

Compound-Complex Sentence

A compound-complex sentence consists of at least two independent clauses and one dependent clause.

Ex. Ashley wanted an eagle for her birthday (independent clause), but because eagles are an endangered species (dependent clause), her parents bought her a turkey instead (independent clause).

Although she wasn't crazy about turkeys (dependent clause), Ashley took the bird under her wing (independent clause), and it became her new best friend (independent clause).

Conjunction

A conjunction shows the logical connections between other words or groups of words. By paying attention to the conjunctions, you can usually see the logical relations between sentences and parts of sentences.

Ex. *And* says that two or more things belong together. (Seth threw a ball, *and* Maggie caught it.)

But shows a contrast between two or more things. (Seth threw a ball, *but* Maggie dropped it.)

Or says that only one of two different things is true. (I will go to the grocery store, *or* I will go to the movies.)

So says that one thing is true because something else is true. (I will go to the grocery store, *so* I will have food to eat tomorrow.)

Contraction

A contraction is a shortened version of a common word combination. When writing a contraction, leave no space between the words and use an apostrophe in place of the missing letters.

Ex. don't (*do not*)
can't (*can not*)
didn't (*did not*)
should've (*should have*)
it's (*it is*)

Coordinating Conjunction

A coordinating conjunction connects words, phrases, or clauses when the words, phrases, or clauses are of equal importance. There are seven coordinating conjunctions that can be memorized by simply remembering: FAN BOYS.

Ex. **For** (Wayne must be flying his kite, for it is the first windy day in weeks.)

And (peas and carrots)

Nor (neither rain nor snow)

But (I love peas, but I do not care for carrots.)

Or (this or that)

Yet (Ashley loves her new turkey, yet it is not exactly the present she had hoped for.)

So (Jason and Jennifer are hungry for Italian food, so they are heading to Little Italy.)

TELL ME MORE!

In the same way that a mechanic needs nuts and bolts to hold his machinery together, so our sentences need certain words to hold them together. Conjunctions are just those kinds of words. They are the words that hold sentences together. Coordinating conjunctions are single words that hold equal parts of sentences together. Besides holding simple sentences together to form compound sentences, coordinating conjunctions can also hold two or more nouns or verbs together.

Independent clauses can also begin with a coordinating conjunction! You may get the feeling that the independent clause is really and truly just as dependent on the clause that came before as is any dependent clause. If you see a sentence that begins, "And _____," you realize something came before. And you probably want to know what came before. But, of course, it is acceptable to begin a simple sentence with *and*, *or*, or *but*.

If you memorize the coordinating conjunctions (FANBOYS—*for*, *and*, *nor*, *but*, *or*, *yet*, *so*), you can figure that any other conjunctions are subordinating conjunctions that begin dependent clauses.

Correlative Conjunctions

Correlative conjunctions are conjunctions that work only in pairs.

Ex. either/or (Maggie wants either the red one or the blue one.)

Neither/ nor (I have neither the money nor the time to invest in this!)

Dash

The dash (—) is a very useful punctuation mark that may best be described as a cross between a comma, a colon, and an ellipsis. The dash is sometimes known as the **em dash**. Here are a few examples of its many functions.

Ex. To indicate a sudden break or change in the sentence. (At the end of her shift—and this was not all her fault—Sarah forgot to clock out.)

To set off an introductory series from its explanation. (A cake, a few close friends, a new turkey—these things made Ashley's birthday special.)

To set off parenthetical material that explains or clarifies a word or a phrase. (My favorite place—the grocery store at the end of the block—changed this neighborhood forever.)

To indicate interrupted speech in a dialog. (I cried, "What is—" "It's a turkey!" exclaimed Ashley.)

To emphasize a word, a series, a phrase, or a clause. (And then I turned around and saw who it was—the butler!)

Declarative Sentence

A declarative sentence gives information. The speaker is making a declaration of what he thinks is true. Declarative sentences end in periods.

Ex. Indian elephants have smaller ears than African elephants.

Definite Article (see Article)

Delayed Subject (see Subject)

Demonstrative Pronoun (see Determiner)

Dependent Clause (see Subordinate Clause)

Descriptive Paragraph

A descriptive paragraph is dedicated primarily to describing something. Descriptive paragraphs paint a clear picture of a person, place, thing, or idea—how it looks, smells, sounds, tastes, and/or feels. Descriptive paragraphs are distinct from, though they may contain elements of, persuasive, expository, or narrative paragraphs. You may find descriptive paragraphs in just about any written work, though they are more common in historical works and works of fiction.

Ex. The turkey clucked in excitement as it escaped from the box. It was the most unique bird Ashley had ever seen. Its long, silky feathers of every color glistened in the light like a sunset. Its sparkling eyes somehow knew her already. As it pranced around the room, it made a peculiar sound that Ashley knew meant Thanksgiving would never be the same again.

Determiner

Determiners, like articles and quantifiers, serve as adjectives and always come immediately before the nouns they modify. **Determiners**, in particular, specify which specific thing (or things) you are talking about. If they are used by themselves, most determiners can also serve as **demonstrative pronouns**.

Ex. *This* aardvark

That badger

These missiles

Those children

This is fantastic! (*This* is also a demonstrative pronoun in this sentence)

I'm not so sure about *that*. (*that* is also a demonstrative pronoun in this sentence)

Diagonal

A diagonal (/), or **slash**, is a mark of punctuation used to create fractions, show choices, or indicate line breaks in poetry.

Ex. Although the recipe called for ½ cup flour, Margaret mistakenly put in 1½ cups.

To change channels, use the up/down button on the remote control.

Roses are red/ violets are blue/ I hope this example/ is helpful to you.

Direct Object

A direct object is a noun that *receives* the action or is *affected by* the action from a subject.

Ex. Zelda kicks a ball. (Zelda is the subject, and *ball* is the direct object.)

TELL ME MORE!

Here are a few more examples. *The ball hit the tree.* Identify the two nouns in this sentence. (*ball* and *tree*) Which of the nouns is the subject of the sentence or, put another way, which noun is doing the action? The ball is the thing that hits, so it is the actor, and therefore, the subject of the sentence. Which noun is the direct object of the sentence, the thing that receives the action or is affected by the action? The tree is the thing being hit, so it is the direct object.

Pharaoh's servants whipped the Israelite slaves. Identify the two nouns in this sentence. (*servants* and *slaves*) NOTE: On its own, *Pharaoh* would be a noun. But *Pharaoh* doesn't stand by itself. In fact, the word is not *Pharaoh*, but *Pharaoh's*. And *Pharaoh's* is followed by another noun: *servants*. The noun *servants* is being modified by the word *Pharaoh's*; so *Pharaoh's* is an adjective and *servants* is the noun. What about *Israelite*; is it a noun? Is *slaves* a noun? (*Slaves* is a noun; *Israelite* is the adjective that describes the slaves.) Which of the nouns is the subject of the sentence? The servants are doing the whipping, so they are the subject of the sentence. Which noun is the direct object of the sentence? The slaves are being whipped, so they are the direct object.

An **object complement** is a noun, pronoun, or adjective that follows a direct object and renames it or tells what the direct object has become.

Ex. The product development department elected me *president*.

Ellipsis

An ellipsis (. . .) is a punctuation mark that looks like three periods in a row. Ellipses (plural for ellipsis) can indicate missing material, a pause, or an incomplete thought.

Ex. To indicate in formal quotations that a portion of the quoted section has been left out. (Original: We the students of Andersen High School, in order to improve our education, do hereby protest. Quotation: "We the students . . . do hereby protest.")

To indicate a pause. (Ashley untied the bow and opened the box. Inside was a . . . could it be . . . yes, it was . . . a turkey!)

To indicate that a speaker didn't finish his sentence. (I just couldn't remember what I was going to . . .)

TELL ME MORE!

Ellipsis pauses are unlike comma, colon, and semicolon pauses, because they do not help the reader understand what the speaker is saying. They do help the reader know how the speaker is saying something, which can shed light on the speaker's meaning and character. Also, when used in quotations, they alert the reader to missing text, which is important to know for academic pursuits.

Ellipses can also indicate a pause: perhaps a speaker, gasping for breath, had to take a break from speaking; maybe he had to think deeply about exactly what word to use next, and so paused in mid-sentence before continuing . . . . Or maybe . . . the author . . . simply . . . wants . . . to slow . . . the reader . . . down. The ellipsis says, "Take note! Things . . . slow . . . down . . . here."

Ellipses at the end of sentences are always preceded by the closing punctuation of the sentence—a period, a question mark, or an exclamation point. It is for this reason that you find four "periods" in a row at the end of sentences. The first period is truly a period; the other three dots are simply parts of an ellipsis.

Em dash (see Dash)

Exclamation Point

An exclamation point (!) is a punctuation mark that goes at the end of an interjection or exclamatory sentence. It communicates strong emotion or surprise.

> Ex. My dog jumped over the fence!

Exclamatory Sentence

An exclamatory sentence is a sentence that communicates strong emotion or surprise and ends with an exclamation point.

> Ex. My neighbor's cat is missing!

Expletive

An expletive is a word or phrase that conveys no independent meaning but merely fulfills a structural function within a sentence. Expletives usually take the form of the word *there* or *it*, followed by some form of the verb *to be*. They are commonly found at the beginning of cleft sentences. See also *Cleft Sentence*.

> Ex. *It was* the papaya that fell off the kitchen table.
> *There were* seven football players who got hurt.

Expository Paragraph

An expository paragraph explains something; it exposes the meaning of something or the reason why. An expository paragraph is meant to convey information or to help the reader's understanding. It is distinct from, though it may contain elements of, a persuasive, narrative, or descriptive paragraph. Even if it is telling a story or describing something, an expository paragraph's primary purpose is explanation.

> Ex. Natural disasters often result in uncommon scientific collaborations. For example, seismologists are geophysics specialists who study earthquakes.

Oceanographers, on the other hand, study the many features of oceans. While these experts in land and sea would normally have little interaction, an undersea earthquake that causes a tsunami—a giant tidal wave—will force them to combine their expertise in order to understand the events.

TELL ME MORE!

As when we dissect an animal, peeling back its skin, muscles and bones to reveal what lies beneath and inside, so the expository paragraph peels back and exposes what is inside a topic of discussion. Encyclopedia articles are almost always made up of purely expository paragraphs. But you'll find expository paragraphs elsewhere as well: in fiction, you may find that the author has a character think something through so that you understand what you (and the character) did not understand before. In non-fiction books, most authors who expose you to new information want to do more than merely teach you something new. They want to convince you that they are correct about some matter. If a paragraph goes beyond merely informing and is obviously written to convince you about a matter, it has a different name.

Foreshadowing

Foreshadowing is a writing technique used to heighten the tension in a story. When using foreshadowing, an author will give hints or clues about what is going to happen later. Those hints and clues give you an inkling of what is to come . . . *before* it actually happens.

> Ex. Michael was finishing his last long run of the week. As he turned the last corner toward home, he sensed that something was different. The cars parked along the street were not the usual ones he remembered seeing on previous trips down this block. (This paragraph gives the reader an inkling that something different is about to occur, probably involving the parked cars.)

Fragment (see Sentence Fragment)

Gerund

A gerund is a noun made from a verb. Gerunds end in *–ing*.

> Ex. I love *singing*.
> *Playing* is fun.
> *Running* back and forth to the store is no fun!

TELL ME MORE!

Gerunds can take objects, just like regular verbs do. They can also be modified by adverbs, just as regular verbs can be modified. If you use a gerund in a sentence, you are writing in the passive voice. Get rid of gerunds whenever possible!

Ex.   Climbing stairs is a lot more difficult than riding an escalator. (The gerund *climbing* takes the object *stairs*, and the gerund *riding* takes the object *escalator*.)

Gerund Phrase

A gerund phrase consists of the gerund itself, plus any adverbs, objects, or other words whose meanings are directly tied to the gerund. A gerund phrase—like the gerund by itself—serves as a noun.

Ex.   Climbing stairs is a lot more difficult than riding an escalator.

Helping Verb

A helping (or **auxiliary**) verb modifies the meaning of a primary verb. It can control verb tenses and express a sense of necessity, certainty, probability, or possibility. See also *Verb Tense*.

Ex.   Seth *had* gone.

Maggie *was* going.

Herman *will* go.

That *might have* meant a lot of trouble for her.

The children *were* taken away. –or- the children *will have to be* taken away.

We *must* go.

Homograph

Homographs are words that are spelled alike but have different meanings. Homographs may or may not sound alike.

Ex.   *bow* (on a package); *bow* (what a violinist uses); *bow* (to shoot an arrow); *bow* (what a violinist does when the audience claps); *bow* (the front part of a boat)

Wind (blowing air); *wind* (what you have to do to the spring of a mechanical watch)

Homonym

In the strict sense, homonyms are words that both sound the same *and* are spelled the same, but do not mean the same thing.

Ex.   *rose* (flower); *rose* (stood up)
fair (carnival); *fair* (reasonable)
bee (insect); *bee* (group of people: quilting *bee*)
saw (cuts wood); *saw* (past tense of "see")

TELL ME MORE!

Homonyms, by definition, are also *homophones* and *homographs*. For example, the homonyms *bow* (on a package) and *bow* (used to shoot an arrow) are homophones because they are two words that sound alike *and* homographs because they are also spelled alike. But not all homophones or homographs are also homonyms. The chart below may help you see the distinction.

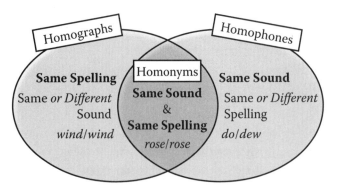

Keep in mind that many use the term *homonym* more loosely, to mean "words that share the same spelling, regardless of pronunciation *or* share the same pronunciation, regardless of spelling." Therefore, you will probably find true homographs like <u>object</u> (a tangible thing) and <u>object</u> (to disagree), and true homophones like *bow* and *bough* classified as homonyms.

Homophones

Homophones are words that sound the same but have different meanings. Homophones may or may not have the same spelling.

Ex.   deer/dear
be/bee
piece/peace

Hyphen

A hyphen is a punctuation mark with multiple uses. It looks like a short dash (-).

Ex.   To divide words between their syllables when they are too long to fit on a single line

To join two or more words in compound numbers (*twenty-four, ninety-nine,* etc.)

To make compound words (*sixteen-year-old* boy)

To join single letters with other words (*T-shirt*)

To join numbers in scores, votes, life spans, etc. (*1865-1903, 24-17*)

To join two or more words that form a single adjective before a noun (*hard-working* man)

To prevent confusion (*re-create* instead of recreate)

Idiom

An idiom is a group of words that paints a mental picture (a "word picture" or "figure of speech") that means something totally different from what the words themselves imply. Some idioms can sound quite silly if you don't recognize them for what they are.

Ex.   Phil was *pulling my leg*. The product development team was *having a ball*.

Imperative

An imperative is a sentence in which one person commands another to do something. When you issue a command, you are saying that it is imperative—necessary—that someone do what you say. The subjects of imperative sentences are usually implied or understood. The subject is almost always you (the person being spoken to).

Ex.   Go to your room!
Tell the doctor what he needs to know.
Go to the zoo to see the elephants.

Implied Subject (see Subject)

Indefinite Article (see Article)

Indefinite Pronoun (see Pronoun)

Indentation

An indentation is an extra space that has been pushed in from the margin toward the middle of the page. Usually, the first line in a paragraph is indented.

Ex.   Although Michael desperately wanted his computer fixed, Ryan decided that the problem was best ignored. Frustrated, but resigned, Michael continued his work. Unfortunately, the problem continued to rear its head. It would not be ignored!

Independent Clause

An independent clause contains a subject and a predicate, conveys a complete thought, and can stand alone as a sentence.

Ex.   Wayne and Sue were too busy to play.
Skeeter goes to school.

Indirect Object

The indirect object of a transitive verb receives the action of the verb indirectly. In other words, it receives the action *after* the direct object receives it and as a *result* of the direct object having received the action.

Ex.   He threw *Fran* the ball. (*Fran* receives the ball as a result of the ball receiving the direct action of being thrown.)

Shelly handed her *son* the keys. (The keys are the direct object; they are what receive the direct action of being handed; Shelly's *son* is the indirect object, because he receives the keys as a result of the keys having received the direct action of being handed.)

NOTE: Although a prepositional phrase may tell you the same information that an indirect object does (Shelly handed the keys *to her son*), a prepositional phrase is never an indirect object. It always remains a prepositional phrase.

Indirect Quotation (see Quotation Marks)

Infinitive

An infinitive is a verb form, usually beginning with the word to, that functions as a noun, adverb, or adjective. Although an infinitive is made from a verb, it does not function as a verb. Infinitives can take objects, just like regular verbs do. They can also be modified by adverbs, just as regular verbs can be modified.

Ex.   To climb those stairs would about kill me. (The infinitive *to climb* takes the object *stairs*.)

I really don't want to drive the car. (The infinitive *to drive* takes the object *car*.)

TELL ME MORE!

Some verbs almost always come together with infinitives. In fact, they don't make sense without infinitives.

Ex.   I <u>used</u> *to go* to the grocery store.
I am <u>going</u> *to buy* a caramel latte.
She <u>has</u> *to eat* the pickle.

We usually think of the verbs that follow *used to*, *going to*, and *has to* as completely separate from the two words that precede them. But you should always interpret the verb that precedes the word to (used, going, has, etc.) as combining with the infinitive (to go, to buy, to eat, etc.) to form what grammarians call a **modal** or **phrasal verb**.

Infinitive Phrase

An infinitive phrase consists of the infinitive itself plus any adverbs, objects, or other words whose meanings are directly tied to the infinitive itself. Like an infinitive, an infinitive phrase can serve as a noun, an adverb, or an adjective, but never as a verb.

Ex.   *To climb those stairs* would about kill me.
I really don't want *to drive the car.*

Initialism (see Abbreviations)

Intensive Pronoun

An intensive pronoun is a pronoun with the suffix -self or -selves. An intensive pronoun intensifies or emphasizes the noun or pronoun to which it refers.

Ex.   Sondra picked the restaurant all by *herself.*
We, *ourselves,* want nothing to do with it!

Interjection

An interjection is a one- or two-word expression of emotion that doesn't communicate significant meaning. It usually ends with an exclamation point, or it can be set off from the rest of a sentence with commas.

Ex.   "*Oh,* I wish I could go on vacation."
"*Wow!* Do you really have a turkey?"

Interrogative Sentence

An interrogative sentence asks a question of (interrogates) the person who hears it. Interrogative sentences always end with question marks.

Ex.   Did you know that Bo's favorite sport is shuffleboard?

Interrogative Pronoun

Interrogative pronouns are pronouns that are used only when asking a question. They include *who, whose, whom, which,* and *what.*

Ex.   *Who* are you?

What do you want?

Whose bright idea was it to let her pick the restaurant?

Intransitive Verb

When a verb has no direct object it is called an intransitive verb. It does not *transfer* (that's where we get that word *transitive*) any action from one noun to another.

Intransitive verbs talk about actions that affect no one and nothing other than the subject itself.

Ex.   Fran *slept.* (You would never ask, "*What* did Fran sleep?" or "*Who* did she sleep?" Those questions don't even make sense! Fran did the sleeping, and the sleeping affected Fran herself.)

John *jumped.* (You don't need to ask, "*What* did John jump?" John did the jumping. His body jumped.)

Italics

Italics is a printing term that refers to type that is slightly slanted. In this sentence, the word *xylophone* is in italics. If you underline handwritten text it is normally set in *italics* when typeset. Italics are usually used for emphasis or ease of identification.

Ex.   To identify titles of books, magazine titles, and album titles. (Michael is reading *The Design of Everyday Things.* Sondra has a subscription to *Bon Appetit.* MercyMe's song "I Can Only Imagine" is on the album *Almost There.*)

To add emphasis to a particular word or phrase. (No wonder you're lost! I told you to take the *right* turn in Albuquerque, not the left.)

To identify words being used. (The word *so* is a coordinating conjunction.)

To show that a word is in a foreign language. (Mix it all up and *voila,* you have a masterpiece.)

Linking Verb

A linking verb describes the way things *are* or *seem to be.* Linking verbs help identify connections between subjects and other nouns or adjectives. The nouns and adjectives to which linking verbs tie their subjects are called predicate nouns and predicate adjectives.

Ex.   Rutabagas *are* bitter. (*are* is the linking verb and *bitter* is the predicate adjective)

Turkeys *are* birds. (*are* is the linking verb and *birds* is the predicate noun)

Water *seems* clear. (*seems* is the linking verb and *clear* is the predicate adjective)

TELL ME MORE!
Notice that besides speaking of things in unmistakably true and unchanging states, there are a number of linking verbs that suggest mere belief or sense that something is true (feel, look, smell, etc. *He looks tall*) or that suggest the situation may be changing (grow, become, stay, etc. *He grew taller*).

A linking verb connects a subject with a noun, no matter how many adjectives modify that noun. The linking verb connects the subject with the predicate noun; it does not connect the subject with the adjectives.

> Ex. The condor *is* a bird. (The linking verb *is* connects the subject, condor, and the predicate noun, bird.)
>
> The condor *is* big. (The linking verb *is* connects the subject, condor, to the predicate adjective, big.)
>
> The condor *is* a big bird. (The adjective *big* and the article *a* refer to and modify our understanding of the noun *bird*. They do not directly refer to the noun *condor*. [We know that they refer to *condor* only because we first know that they refer to *bird*.] The linking verb *is* connects the subject, condor, to the predicate noun, bird. The fact that the predicate includes two adjectives as well does not alter the fact that the sentence includes a predicate noun and not any predicate adjectives.)

Linking verbs are relatively weak verbs because—as their names explain—they simply link; they don't do anything! Whenever possible, you should replace linking verbs with active verbs—verbs that actually do something. Sentences with active verbs are much more enjoyable to read. Common linking verbs include the following: are, am, appear, stay, was, small, sound, look, were, seem, taste, turn, be, grow, feel, get, been, become, and remain.

Margin

The margin is the space around the outside edges of a sheet of paper beyond the printed area.

> Ex. This page you are reading has top, bottom, left, and right margins.

Metaphor

A metaphor is an analogy that compares two different things using imaginative phrases to make them seem the same when they are really different. Instead of being directly compared, though, one thing is actually said to be another. In each case, the statement is not literally true, but it communicates something that is true in a powerful way. The reader is expected to interpret what the truth is.

> Ex. She is ice. (Is she frozen in water? No, but she is cold!)
>
> He was a rock. (Is he an actual rock? No, but his muscles are solid and hard!)

TELL ME MORE!

A metaphor compares two things, but doesn't tell us it is making a comparison. We have to figure that out.

Metaphors help readers to understand and remember better what, exactly, an author is talking about. They help us form pictures in our minds. The phrase, "A man's home is his castle," is an example of a metaphor. Clearly, most men's homes (your father's home, for example!) are not castles. So what does this phrase mean? It means a man's home is *supposed* to be a place of refuge, a place of protection from outside pressures.

David used a metaphor when he said that "[God's] word is a lamp to my feet and a light to my path" (Psalm 119:105).

Is God's word truly a lamp? Does it produce physical light? No. But it is like a lamp, isn't it? If you were to think of your life as being like a path, then God's word is like a lamp. God's word helps you to see your way through life.

Here is another biblical example of a metaphor. Jesus said, "I am the vine; you are the branches; if a man remains in me and I in him, he will bear much fruit" (John 15:5). Clearly, Jesus was not (and is not) a fruit vine. And neither you nor I nor anyone else Jesus was talking to were or are branches on a vine. None of us produces grapes. But there is a sense in which what Jesus said is true. Isn't it true that in the same way a branch must remain connected to the grape vine if it is to bear fruit, so, too, we must remain connected to Jesus if our lives are to be fruitful?

Advertisers often use metaphors to market their products. Red Bull claims their energy beverage is "the drink that gives you wings." This is a metaphor, because it is not telling you Red Bull is *like* having wings or is *as good as* having wings, but rather that it *gives you wings*. Obviously, Red Bull does not literally give you wings. But the makers of Red Bull want you to think of their drink as uplifting and energizing. Likewise, the advertisements for the Yellow Pages say you should, "let your fingers do the walking™." They don't mean you should stand on your hands and walk upside-down on your fingers. They mean that if you use the yellow pages you can discover what you need with your fingers, so you don't have to walk around town to find it.

Besides helping us to "see" what they are talking about, authors can use metaphors to cause readers to *think more deeply* about things. Indeed, metaphors can impart deeper significance. Orthodox and Roman Catholic Christians, for instance, say Jesus' statement at the Last Supper, "this is My Body. . . this is My Blood," is to be understood literally (at Communion the bread and the wine actually become Jesus' body and blood). Protestants say Jesus' statement is to be understood metaphorically or symbolically. Even if the Protestants' interpretation is correct, no Protestant would want to suggest that Jesus was setting up a simple analogy: "this bread is like My Body" or "this wine is like My Blood." They would say Jesus meant something more, something deeper. Exactly what He was saying, exactly how deep was His symbolism and how obscure His metaphor: that is a matter of great debate.

Meter

Meter is the "beat" of a piece of writing. Poetry, for example, can feature many different types of patterned repetition of stressed and unstressed syllables, giving poems a "feel" that often complements what their words express.

Ex. Many of Dr. Seuss' books feature delightful meter as a primary element.

Modal Verb (see Phrasal Verb)

Narrative Paragraph

A narrative paragraph tells a story; it expresses what happened. It is distinct from, though it may contain elements of, a persuasive, expository, or descriptive paragraph.

Ex. Martha shut the door. She couldn't believe this was happening. What would the others think? She turned the key and locked the deadbolt. Stooping, she slid the key through the mail slot at the bottom of the door. With a tear in her eye, she turned and walked down the stairs for the last time.

Negative Statement

A negative statement expresses that something is not true. Negative statements usually feature words such as *no, not, nothing,* or *no one.*

Ex. I am *not* hot.
There is *nothing* to see here.
We have *no* more money.

TELL ME MORE!
No and *not* can also be adjectives or adverbs that modify nouns, adjectives, verbs, or other adverbs.

Ex. Modifying an adjective: That is *not* a cold duck. (Negating cold)

Modifying a noun: That is *not* a duck. (Negating duck)

Modifying a verb: He is *not* flying. (Negating flying)

Modifying an adverb: He's *not* flying high. (Negating high)

Nonrestrictive Clause or Phrase

A nonrestrictive clause or phrase adds information that is interesting but not essential to the meaning of a sentence. You can tell that a clause is nonrestrictive if the meaning of the sentence does not change when you remove it. When you include a nonrestrictive clause or phrase, surround it by commas.

Ex. I smiled, *resting a weary arm on my friend's shoulder.* (The phrase *resting a weary arm on my friend's shoulder* certainly adds information, but it is not essential to understanding the message of the sentence: I smiled.)

In my house, *small as it is,* I can't hear the kids when they are in the basement. (That the house is small is interesting, but does not affect the meaning of the sentence: I can't hear the kids when they are in the basement.)

TELL ME MORE!
There is often confusion about the proper usage of the words *that* and *which. That* should be used at the beginning of restrictive clauses, while *which* should be used at the beginning of nonrestrictive clauses.

Ex. The ape *that* attacked the child was caught yesterday.

The ape, *which* many people find repulsive, is a jungle dweller.

Non-vocalized Sounds

A non-vocalized sound is created when you say a word and/or create sound without using your vocal chords. You can tell if a sound is non-vocalized by placing your fingertips on your throat.

Ex. Say the /p/ or /k/ sound. You should feel no vibrations. Sometimes the suffix *-ed* is non-vocalized (it sounds like /t/—as in fixed).

Noun

Nouns are the most important parts of speech to understand. **Nouns** name people, places, things, or ideas. The first word you ever learned was probably a noun—maybe a person (*Mama* or *Dada*) or a favorite toy (*Pooh*). Nouns come in three forms: proper, common, and pronouns. Proper nouns are names; common nouns speak of the general kind of thing that proper nouns name; pronouns are used in place of proper and common nouns.

Ex. People: man (common noun); Phil (proper noun); him (pronoun)

Places: city (common noun); Denver (proper noun); Paraguay (proper noun)

Things: boat (common noun); *Queen Mary* (proper noun); it (pronoun)

Ideas, concepts, or feelings: love (common noun); freedom (common noun)

TELL ME MORE!

Nouns have many functions. For example, nouns can operate in a sentence as: subjects, direct objects, indirect objects, objects of prepositions, appositives, or predicate nouns. Each of these functions is described in greater detail in its own section of this appendix.

Nouns of Direct Address

A noun of direct address identifies to whom one is speaking. Always use commas to set off **nouns of direct address** from the rest of the sentence in which they appear.

Ex. "*Mom*, do I have to?"
"Of course, *Karleen*, you know you have to."
"Would you like fries with that, *Mr. Ballard*?"

Numerals

Numbers can either be spelled out (four, nine) or written as numerals (4, 9). There are many rules that govern when to use words and when to use numerals.

Ex. For numbers one to nine, use words; for numbers 10 & above, use numerals.

Use a combination for large numbers (7.9 trillion).

Maintain consistency if numbers are being compared or contrasted (four to ten or 4 to 10).

Use numerals for statistics, decimals, pages, chapters, and identifications (33%, 14.7, page 3, chapter 6, 555-1234, 14 Memory Lane, January 13, 1971, A.D. 36)

Use words for numbers at the start of a sentence (Twelve students are absent today).

For time and money, use numerals if abbreviations or symbols are used, but use words if spelled out (3:30 P.M., six o'clock, fifty dollars, $100).

Object (see Direct Object or Indirect Object)

Object Complement (see Direct Object)

Object of the Preposition

The object of a preposition is the noun or pronoun whose meaning is attached to a preposition, i.e., the noun or pronoun helping to complete the meaning of the preposition. The preposition and the object of the preposition, together, form a prepositional phrase.

Ex. Up the *chimney* (Up is the preposition: it establishes direction; *chimney* is the object of the preposition: it tells us where the subject went up.)

Across the *bay* (Across is the preposition: it establishes direction; *bay* is the object of the preposition: it tells us where or what the subject went across.)

Onomatopoeia

Onomatopoeia means a word that imitates the sound it represents.

Ex. splash, buzz, purr, boom, crash

Palindrome

A palindrome is a word, or group of words, that spells the same thing frontward and backward.

Ex. mom, pop, sis, gag, race car, Stanley Yelnats

Paragraph

A paragraph is a group of sentences that convey a common idea or hold together in a logical manner. For example, a paragraph of dialog may not even include a complete thought, but it holds together logically, because it conveys the complete expression of one speaker. A paragraph may consist of just a couple of sentences or hundreds of sentences. Paragraphs are set apart from one another either by indenting the first line of each paragraph by four or five spaces or placing extra space between them.

Ex. Duane really missed off-roading. Even though he loved his minivan, he longed for the days when he could attack a backwoods trail and see sights reserved for the truly adventurous. Perhaps his wife would buy him a new four-wheel-drive vehicle for his birthday. What a gift that would be!

TELL ME MORE!

Four or five hundred years ago, you could find authors who wrote single sentences that lasted a full page or more; they would then write paragraphs that lasted for several pages. Nowadays, you would be hard-pressed to find a well-known author who writes sentences that are longer than three or four lines or paragraphs that are longer than half a page at the most. In most books, you will find at least two paragraphs per page, and, generally, four, five, six, or more.

Unfortunately, there really is no definition of a paragraph that *always* makes sense and will *always* help you to write more effectively. There is a general guideline, though, that will help you decide whether you're looking at a good paragraph or not: a well-written paragraph hangs together *visually* and it hangs together *logically*.

Visually: Paragraphs are groups of sentences. In each paragraph, the sentences are strung end to end: after the final punctuation of one sentence, there is a space, and then the next sentence begins. Because of the way English is written, and because of the manner in which words are printed on a page, paragraphs are laid out in blocks, with a left margin and a right margin: a line on the left and a line on the right beyond which no letters are written.

The first character of the first sentence in a paragraph is normally indented four or five characters from the left margin. Otherwise, every line begins at the same spot on the left margin. While the left margin forms a perfectly straight line, and every line begins at the same spot relative to the left edge of the page, the right margin is usually more ragged: the lines extend to within a few spaces on either side of a vertical line down the right-hand side of the page (or column). Some people add a little bit of vertical space *between* paragraphs. That is what holds paragraphs together *visually*.

Logically: What causes paragraphs to hang together *logically* is not as clear. Logically, a paragraph should be a set of sentences about "the same subject." But what does that mean? An entire *book* is normally about one topic! The question is: how *big* a topic should one cover within a single paragraph? And there is more! What if you are not really writing about a *subject*, but you're telling a *story*? Or what if you're recounting a conversation between two people? What if you're trying to present an *argument*? . . .

Paragraph Break

A paragraph break indicates a separation between paragraphs or a transition to a new paragraph.

    Ex.   When different speakers talk to one another, each person's speech is placed in its own paragraph, thereby requiring frequent paragraph breaks.

Parentheses

Parentheses [( )] are marks of punctuation used to set off additional explanatory material that might otherwise disrupt regular sentence structure.

    Ex.   Kaitlyn (my dog) loves to play in the snow. When different speakers talk to one another, each person's speech is placed in its own paragraph, thereby requiring frequent paragraph breaks.

Parenthetical Expression

A **parenthetical expression** is a remark that has been inserted into another thought, but does not directly deal with the topic at hand. They can appear in the midst of or between sentences. Shorter parentheticals are set off by commas, but longer expressions may be set off by dashes or parentheses. For example:

    Ex.   My dad—*your grandpa*—is a very funny man.

           Of course, that will only start to stink if you open it.

           Yesterday, I ran a mile *(even though I prefer to swim)* and finished 100 crunches.

Participial Phrase

A participial phrase consists of a participle plus any helping verbs, adverbs, objects, or other words whose meanings are directly tied to the participle. Participial phrases, like participles, serve as adjectives.

    Ex.   *Eating her lunch*, Kelly discovered a worm in an apple. (the participle *eating* takes the direct object *lunch* and modifies the proper noun *Kelly*)

           Having hit the sack at 10 o'clock, Pam was ready to milk the cows at dawn. (the participle *having hit* takes the object *sack* and modifies the proper noun *Pam*)

Participle

A participle is a verb that acts as an adjective. These verbs most often end with *-ing* or *-ed*. Since participles are verbs that act like adjectives, they are sometimes called verbal adjectives.

    Ex.   *Climbing* equipment can be expensive!
           Ryan fell into the *churning* water.
           Jay thinks that thunder is *terrifying*.

TELL ME MORE!
Participles can take objects, just like regular verbs do. They can also be modified by helping verbs and adverbs,

just as regular verbs can be modified. Participles are good indicators of passive sentences. Try to eliminate the passive voice whenever possible! See Voice.

Ex. *Eating her lunch*, Kelly discovered a worm in an apple. (the participle *eating* takes the direct object *lunch* and modifies the proper noun *Kelly*)

Having hit the sack at 10 o'clock, Pam was ready to milk the cows at dawn. (the participle *having hit* takes the object *sack* and modifies the proper noun *Pam*)

Passive Voice (see Voice)

Past Tense (see Verb Tense)

Perfect Tense (see Verb Tense)

Period

The period (.) is the mark of punctuation used at the end of sentences that make a statement, request, or mild command. It is also used after abbreviations or initials and as a decimal.

Ex. The aardvark is Phil's favorite animal.

Mr. Whelan entered the U.S. at exactly 9:42 p.m.

The population of Bolinville is about 1.2 million people.

Personification

Personification means giving an inanimate object human qualities.

Ex. The wind moaned and breathed, speaking to all that winter is here.

The sun smiled on the park, calling children from all around to come and play.

Persuasive Paragraph

A persuasive paragraph seeks to convince (persuade) its audience that something is true or that a particular viewpoint is preferred. Persuasive paragraphs are distinct from, though they may contain elements of, narrative, expository, or descriptive paragraphs.

Ex. Our state should have a mandatory seatbelt law. Using seatbelts has proven to be a powerful factor in reducing traffic-related fatalities and injuries. Plus, it is a sad, but proven fact that some people will simply not do certain things in their best interest unless forced to do so.

TELL ME MORE!

Have you ever seen a truly convincing or persuasive *paragraph*? Plenty of paragraphs are parts of much longer persuasive essays. But it's pretty tough to persuade someone with only one paragraph! Still, some paragraphs are obviously meant to *persuade* rather than merely *explain* or *expose*.

Phrasal Verb

A phrasal (or modal) verb is a verb that requires another word—a helping verb, an infinitive, or a prepositional adverb—in order to make sense.

Ex. That coat *stands out*. (Coats don't stand. The preposition out is part of the phrasal verb *stand out*.)

They *get along* well together. (The sentence has no direct object for them to get. The preposition *along* is a part of the phrasal verb *get along*.)

The criminal was *picked up* by the police. (*Up* and *by* are both prepositions; but *up* does not indicate, as you might expect, a direction. Here, the preposition *up* is a part of the phrasal verb *picked up*.)

NOTE: Sometimes the direct object of a phrasal verb (the thing that the phrasal verb affects) may come between the base verb and the preposition: *Hand over* the keys. –or– *Hand* them *over*.

Phrase

A phrase is a group of words that is missing a subject, a predicate, or both. Together, these words express meaning within a clause or sentence. Phrases commonly fulfill the function of a single word—a noun, a verb, an adjective, or an adverb, etc. A phrase always has two or more words but is never a complete sentence.

Ex. *Chasing the cat* is a participial phrase in which *the cat* is the object of the participle *chasing*, and the participle *chasing* is, by definition, an adjective. There is no subject or predicate.

Under the bridge is a prepositional phrase that could be used in a sentence as an adjective to describe where something is or as an adverb to describe where something is occurring.

Running from the law is a gerund phrase that could be used as the subject of a sentence.

Plural

Plural means there is more than one of something. Usually, plurals are formed by adding s to the singular version of a noun. However, there are many exceptions to this rule.

Ex.   Mr. Meyers has one *dog*. We have three *dogs*.

John has a *child* named Amy. Jason has three *children* named Jonathan, Julia, and Jenna.

Sarah grabbed one *tomato*. Old Man Jenkins stuffed four *tomatoes* into his bag.

I need a *dish*! The *dishes* are over there.

Waiter! There's a *fly* in my soup! Get over it. There are *flies* everywhere in here.

This *donkey* won't move. Well, *donkeys* are known for being stubborn.

My name is *Abby*. There are three *Abbys* in my class.

I love my *wife*. The *wives* of pastors must be very patient people.

My *roof* is leaking. After the hurricane, all the *roofs* in town are leaking.

I love my pet *goose*. He stays with me even when all the other *geese* fly south for the winter.

My *brother-in-law* used to live in a yurt. You can never have too many *brothers-in-law*.

My teacher gave us a *quiz* today. She has given us three *quizzes* this week!

Possessive Noun

A possessive noun—meaning that it owns something else—will end with an apostrophe-s ('s) or s-apostrophe (s').

Ex.   *Matt and Jean's* pig (the pig belongs to Matt and Jean)

Ms. Andersen's armadillo (the armadillo belongs to Ms. Andersen)

The *books'* covers (the covers are owned by more than one book)

Bess's cow (the cow belongs to Bess)

Mr. Hernandez's speakers (the speakers belong to Mr. Hernandez)

TELL ME MORE!

What if someone says *Andy's* ten? Does that mean "the ten belongs to Andy"? Yes, if it's a $10 bill. More likely, it is a contraction meaning "Andy is ten."

Also be aware that, although things may sound similar, the possessive changes the meaning:

Ex.   The chipmunks are playing. (more than one chipmunk is playing)

The chipmunk's asleep. (one chipmunk is asleep)

The squirrel is eating the chipmunk's food. (the food belongs to the chipmunk)

I found the chipmunks' house. (the house belongs to the chipmunks)

When more than one person in a series owns something, only attach the apostrophe-s ('s) to the last person.

Ex.   Randy and Tim's aardvark ran away. (the aardvark is owned by both of them)

Randy's and Tim's aardvarks love to play together. (each owns his own aardvark)

Possessive Pronoun

A possessive pronoun is a special form of pronoun that shows possession. To make a possessive pronoun, do not add an apostrophe-s ('s) or an s-apostrophe (s') to the root pronoun. Instead, use a special form of the pronoun.

Ex.   If I own something, it is my thing, or *mine*.
If we own something, it is our thing, or *ours*.
If you own something, it is your thing, or *yours*.
If he owns something, it is his thing, or *his*.
If she owns something, it is her thing, or *hers*.
If it owns something, it is its thing, or *its*.
If they own something, it is their thing, or *theirs*.

NOTE: Do not use apostrophes on any possessive pronoun. None. Never. Do not ever add an apostrophe to any possessive pronoun!

Predicate

The predicate is everything other than the subject in a clause. Every clause or sentence has a predicate. The predicate tells you about the subject: what the subject did, what happened to it, or what it "is." A predicate must always include a verb. In fact, the simplest predicate is a verb all by itself. The verb, by itself, is called the *simple* predicate. A *compound* predicate is one in which there are two or more simple predicates. The *complete* predicate is everything other than the complete subject in a clause, i.e., the *simple* or *compound* predicate plus all its modifiers.

Ex.   **Simple:** Boa constrictors *slither*.

Compound: Boa constrictors *slither* through the jungle and *squeeze* unsuspecting prey.

Complete: Boa constrictors *sleep for hours at a time*.

TELL ME MORE!

You will often find clauses in which the predicate is merely *understood*: Pamela asked, "Would you please bring me a glass of water?" "I might," Philip replied. We know what Philip means, but his sentence does not include the complete predicate: "I might *bring you a glass of water.*" The predicate is implied.

Predicate Adjective

A predicate adjective is an adjective that comes after a linking verb and modifies or describes the subject of a sentence. See also *Linking Verb.*

Ex. Rutabagas are *bitter.* (*are* is the linking verb; *bitter* is the predicate adjective)

Water seems *clear.* (*seems* is the linking verb; *clear* is the predicate adjective)

Predicate Noun

A predicate noun is a noun that comes after a linking verb and defines or describes the subject of a sentence. See also *Linking Verb.*

Ex. Frogs are *amphibians.* (*are* is the linking verb; *amphibians* is the predicate noun)

Turkeys are *birds.* (*are* is the linking verb; *birds* is the predicate noun)

Prefix

A prefix is a letter combination added to the beginning of a root word to change its meaning. Think of prefixes as the letters before ("pre") the root word.

Ex. *Un-*, when added to a root word, reverses its meaning. (Someone can *do* something, and someone else can *undo* it. One person may say an idea is *important*, and someone else may say it's *unimportant.*)

Im- has a similar effect. (One person may think that something is *possible*, but another may believe it's *impossible.*)

Preposition

A preposition tells you *where*, *when*, or *how* something takes place. Most prepositions indicate direction or position (notice the word *position* within the word *preposition*).

Ex. on, at, in, around, through, towards, away from, under, over, up, down, behind

Christian was a waiter *at* the hotel.

Sandy found a half dollar *in* the sand.

Wanda went *to* her friend's house.

Four prepositions—*of*, *by*, *for*, and *with*—don't indicate direction or position. However, they speak of *logical relations* between things.

Ex. Life is like a box *of* chocolates.

Friends are *for* life.

I will stand *by* you.

Randy went to Mexico *with* Linda.

TELL ME MORE!

Prepositions normally require an object—a noun—called the object of the preposition. The object of the preposition tells you the *cause* of the action or *where* it takes place (or *by whom* or *what* it happens). Some prepositions consist of more than one word. Many of these multi-word prepositions include the word *of*.

Ex. because of, in front of, to the side of

Besides standing at the heads of prepositional phrases, prepositions often modify verbs. Grammarians speak of these verb-modifying prepositions as either adverbs or parts of phrasal verbs. Prepositions serve as adverbs when there is no object of the preposition.

Ex. Kristen put the coffee cup *down.*
She looked *up.*

Prepositional Phrase

A prepositional phrase is a phrase that includes the preposition, its object, and any words—adjectives and/ or adverbs—that modify the object. Prepositional phrases almost always serve as adjectives or adverbs. You can save yourself a lot of time when you're trying to figure out the parts of a sentence if you identify the prepositional phrases first.

Ex. The dog ran *up the ladder.* (*Up* is the preposition; it shows a direction or relationship in space or time; *ladder* is the object of the preposition. *Up the ladder* is the prepositional phrase. The phrase as a whole serves as an adverb because it modifies the verb *ran*. It tells where the dog ran.)

Ken called *in the dark.* (*In* is the preposition; it shows a position in space or time; *dark* is the object of the preposition. *In the dark* is the prepositional phrase that serves as an adverb, because it modifies the verb *called*. It tells where Ken called.)

TELL ME MORE!

You will probably be able to "feel" when a preposition doesn't belong in a prepositional phrase. The words that you would think should form the phrase won't "make sense" together. They certainly won't act as adjectives or adverbs!

> Ex. In the sentence *The dog ran up the ladder, up the ladder* makes sense as a prepositional phrase, because it also makes sense as an adverb: the phrase tells you where to run.

But in the sentence *Hand over the keys, over the keys* makes no sense as a prepositional phrase, because it doesn't modify or explain the verb *hand*. However, *the keys* makes sense as the direct object of the phrasal verb *hand over*. Indeed, if *the keys* was not part of this phrase or clause, we would be hard-pressed to know what the person was supposed to *hand* or *hand over*. We need a direct object, and if *the keys* is supposed to be the object of the preposition *over* rather than the direct object of the verbal phrase *hand over*, we have real problems!

If you find a prepositional phrase at the head of a sentence, it can serve as a noun as well, but writing this way is discouraged.

> Ex. *During communion* is not a good time to talk.
> *Back on the farm* is where I long to be.

Present Tense (see Verb Tense)

Pronoun

A pronoun is a noun substitute, i.e., it takes the place of a common noun or proper noun.

> Ex. he, him, his, she, her, hers, it, its, they, them, their, theirs, we, you, I, us, me

TELL ME MORE!

You must use a common or proper noun before you use a pronoun. The noun or pronoun to which a pronoun refers is called the pronoun's antecedent. All pronouns require clear antecedents.

> Ex. Christian likes to wear pink shirts. People tell him the color doesn't look good on him, but he doesn't care. (Christian is the clear antecedent of the pronouns him and he in the second sentence. There is no confusion here.)

Here is an example of poor pronoun usage: *Bruce and Alex* were talking. Bruce said *he* could marry Vivian, because *he* didn't mind if Vivian didn't like *him*. (There is no way of knowing what the writer means each time the word *he* or *him* is used in the second sentence. The pronouns [*he* and *him*] do not have clear antecedents that tell the reader who "he" is.)

Relative pronouns connect (relate) phrases or clauses to nouns or other pronouns. The most common relative pronouns are *who, whoever, which,* and *that.*

> Ex. The anteater *who* runs the fastest usually wins the race.

Indefinite pronouns are pronouns that refer to nothing in particular. The most common indefinite pronouns are *everybody, anybody, somebody, all, each, every, some, none,* and *one.*

> Ex. *Everybody* was excited about the big anteater race.

Pronoun—Case

Each personal pronoun has three cases:

1. Nominative (naming)—when the pronoun is the *subject* of a sentence (I, we, you, he, she, it, they)

2. Objective—when the pronoun is the *object* of the sentence (me, us, you, him, her, it, them)

3. Possessive—when the pronoun *owns* something (my, mine, our, your, his, her, its, their).

Pronouns				
Person/Number	Nominative/Subject	Possessive		Objective/Object
1st/Singular	**I** went to school.	This is **my** house.	This house of **mine**.	That soaked **me**.
1st/Plural	**We** went to school.	This is **our** house.	This house of **ours**.	That soaked **us**.
2nd/Singular	**You** went to school.	This is **your** house.	This house of **yours**.	That soaked **you**.
2nd/Plural	**You** went to school.	This is **your** house.	This house of **yours**.	That soaked **you**.
3rd/Singular Masc	**He** went to school.	This is **his** house.	This house of **his**.	That soaked **him**.
3rd/Singular Fem	**She** went to school.	This is **her** house.	This house of **hers**.	That soaked **her**.
3rd/Singular Neut	**It** went to school.	This is **its** house.		That soaked **it**.
3rd/Plural	**They** went to school.	This is **their** house.	This house of **theirs**.	That soaked **them**.

Ex. The table below shows the correct pronouns to use depending on the case, person, and number of the noun:

NOTE: Except for the neuter, you cannot substitute the first and third person nominative and objective cases. For example, you can't say, "My mom gave *I* (nominative case) a dollar." You have to say, "My mom gave *me* (objective case) a dollar."

Pronoun—Person

The person of a pronoun gives more information about the pronoun. When two people are communicating, whoever is speaking is called the ***first person***, whoever is being spoken to is called the ***second person***, and anyone or anything being spoken about is called the ***third person***.

Ex. First person: *I, me, my/mine, we, us, our/ours* (only people who are talking use these pronouns)

Second person: *you, your, yours* (a speaker will use these words only to refer to the person[s] to whom he is speaking)

Third person: *he, him, his, she, her, hers, they, them, their/theirs, it, its* (except in very strange circumstances, a person will use these words to refer only to people or objects that are not part of the conversation)

Proper Noun

A proper noun is the name of a particular person, place, or thing.

Ex. *Winston Churchill* (proper) (a corresponding common noun would be *man*)

San Francisco (proper) (a corresponding common noun would be *city*)

Denver Nuggets (proper) (a corresponding common noun would be *team*)

Punctuation

A punctuation mark is a symbol used within or at the end of a sentence to clarify meaning.

Ex. comma (,)
period (.)
exclamation point (!)
question mark (?)
colon (:)
semicolon (;)
hyphen (-)
dash (—)
quotation marks (" ")
apostrophe (')

brackets ([ ])
parentheses ( )

Quantifier

A quantifier is a special adjective that always comes immediately before the noun it modifies. Quantifiers tell us how many or how much of a thing we're talking about.

Ex. *Twenty* bags of flour.
No papayas.
A *few* cordless screwdrivers.
All the bed bugs.

TELL ME MORE!
If they are used by themselves, most quantifiers can serve as pronouns.

Ex. There are *none* left.
I own about *twenty*.
Hey! I said I wanted *two*!

Question Mark

The question mark (?) is the punctuation mark used at the end of a sentence that asks a direct question. It can also be used within parentheses to indicate uncertainty. Sentences with question marks are called interrogative.

Ex. Where is my armadillo?

The armadillo is the fastest (?) mammal native to Arizona.

Quotation Marks

Quotation marks (" ") are marks of punctuation used to indicate *exactly* what someone said. Quotation marks are placed immediately before and after what was said. If the words aren't being quoted exactly as they were spoken, then they should not be placed inside quotation marks.

Ex. Maggie said, "Give me the ball, Seth."
Maggie asked Seth to give her the ball.

Quotation marks are also used for titles of certain works and to set off special words or phrases.

Ex. "Like A Rolling Stone" (song title)

Pam is not allowed to use the phrase "bling bling" around her teenage daughter.

TELL ME MORE!
All end punctuation (commas, periods, question marks, etc.) must be placed inside (before) the closing quotation mark.

Ex. "Come to the baseball game," he said. "You'll have a great time."

If the quotation is a question, the question mark should come inside the closing quotation mark. If, however, the quotation itself is not a question, but you are asking a question about the quotation, then the question mark is placed outside of the quotation mark.

Ex.   "Am I dreaming?"

Did she really hear him say "You must have been dreaming"?

Similarly, with exclamation points, if the quotation itself is an exclamation, then the exclamation point is placed inside the final quotation mark. If the quotation is not an exclamation, but you are exclaiming about the quotation, then the exclamation point should come outside the quote.

Ex.   "You are amazing!"

Imagine, he couldn't remember her saying "You are amazing"!

The phrase that indicates who said whatever it is you're quoting—*Daren said*, *Jenny yelled*, etc.—is called the attribution. (See *Attribution*.)

A regular quotation is enclosed within regular, double quotation marks (" "). If the person being quoted then quotes someone else, the quote he is quoting is enclosed within single quotation marks (' '). If this quote-within-a-quote should happen also to include a quote, this third quote-within-a-quote-within-a-quote will be enclosed within double quotes once more . . . and so the pattern would continue.

If you modify the words that someone said in any way your quotation is called an **indirect quotation**. You will not use quotation marks to indicate indirect quotations.

Ex.   There are two common ways authors modify indirect quotations:

They change the tense of the verbs from present to past. Instead of writing, *Chicken Little yelled, "The sky is falling!"* (present tense: the sky *is* falling), they will write, *Chicken Little yelled that the sky was falling* (past tense: the sky *was* falling).

They shift the person of the pronouns, rephrasing what would have been, originally, a first-person reference into a second-person reference. Instead of writing, *Chicken Little yelled, "I'm sure the sky is falling!"* (first-person: *I'm* sure), they will write, *Chicken Little yelled that she was sure the sky was falling* (third-person: *she was* sure).

Reflexive Pronoun

A reflexive pronoun is a pronoun with the *-self* or *-selves* suffix. A reflexive pronoun is used as the object of a sentence when referring back to the subject of the sentence.

Ex.   Randy hurt *himself*.
Linda talks to *herself*.

Relative Clause (see Clause)

Relative Pronoun (see Pronoun)

Restrictive Clause or Phrase

A restrictive clause or phrase adds information that is essential to the meaning of a sentence. Unlike with a nonrestrictive clause or phrase, you should not set off a restrictive clause or phrase with commas, parentheses, dashes, or any other punctuation that might set it apart from the rest of the sentence.

Ex.   Customers *with strollers* may not use the escalator. (If you remove the phrase *with strollers*, the meaning of the sentence would change.)

You can't get there *from here*. (The meaning of this sentence changes if you remove the restrictive phrase *from here*. Without that essential phrase, the sentence would mean, simply, you can't get there at all!)

TELL ME MORE!

Some appositives, however, are restrictive; they narrow or focus the meaning of the noun they are renaming or describing. You should not surround restrictive appositives with commas.

Ex.   My favorite is the author *Robert Ludlum*.

The band *Relient K* just produced its first gold album.

I think his ferret *Hildegard* is spoiled.

There is often confusion about the proper usage of the words that and which. That should be used at the beginning of restrictive clauses, while which should be used at the beginning of nonrestrictive clauses.

Ex.   The ape *that* attacked the child was caught yesterday.

The ape, *which* many people find repulsive, is a jungle dweller.

Rhetorical Question

A rhetorical question is a question for which no answer is expected because the answer is so obvious or is simply not required.

Ex.   Are you kidding?
Can you believe it?

Rhyme

Rhyme is a term used to describe words with endings that sound very similar. Words do not need to be spelled similarly in order to rhyme; they only need to sound the same.

Ex. hiking/biking
mad/dad
red/bed/head

Root Word

Although many words come in different forms, each word has a root or core meaning. We can add parts—suffixes and/or prefixes—to the root word to change its meaning.

Ex. *want*: wants, wanting, wanted
blink: blinks, blinking, blinked
snow: snows, snowing, snowed

Semicolon

The semicolon (;) is a punctuation mark that acts like a weak period or a strong comma. The semicolon acts as a weak period when it replaces the period at the end of one sentence and stitches that sentence together with the next to form a single sentence. It acts as a strong comma by clearly showing the breaks between the members of a series (especially when one [or more] of the clauses or phrases in a series already contains commas).

Ex. I did not call myself a musician; I told people that I played the guitar. (joining two or more independent clauses that are not connected with a coordinating conjunction)

I never forget to bring my beach gear when I go to the ocean—sun block, visor, and sunglasses; snorkel, fins, and water wings; towel, bathing suit, and flip flops. (separating groups of words that already contain commas)

Sentence

A sentence is a group of words that (1) has a subject (who or what the sentence is about), (2) has a predicate (a verb) that tells you something about the subject, and (3) expresses a complete thought. A sentence, then, will usually have at least two words. There are two other important rules about sentences: (1) a sentence *always* begins with a capital letter; and (2) a sentence *always* ends with a closing punctuation mark—either a period, a question mark, or an exclamation point.

Ex. Karleen ran.
Warren jumped over the river!
Did Margaret fall in the pool?

TELL ME MORE!

Sentences come in four basic structures: simple, compound, complex, and compound-complex. Each sentence is designed to fulfill one of four functions: declarative, imperative, interrogative, or exclamatory. Occasionally, you may see one-word sentences. One-word sentences *always* occur in the midst of other sentences. They don't make any sense on their own, so the sentences that surround them must supply the missing meanings.

Ex. "Hey!" or "Wow!" or "Really?" or "Run!"

Sentence Fragment

A sentence fragment is one or more words that do not form a complete thought punctuated as a sentence. It is not a complete sentence, because it is missing a subject, a predicate, or both. A sentence fragment may also be a subordinate clause.

Ex. Penguins across the ice. (The sentence fragment is a missing a verb. Adding a verb will make it a complete sentence: Penguins *skated* across the ice.)

When the Zamboni was finished. (This sentence fragment is a subordinate clause. Adding an independent clause will make it a complete sentence: When the Zamboni was finished, *penguins skated across the ice.*)

Spinning and doing pirouettes. The penguins rocked the house. (The sentence fragment Spinning and doing pirouettes is followed by a complete sentence. The two can be joined to form one complete sentence: Spinning and doing pirouettes, the penguins rocked the house.)

Simile

A simile is an analogy that compares two things that are not obviously similar and suggests there are similarities. Similes use the word *like* or *as*.

Ex. Marie was *stiff <u>as</u> a board.*
Ed was *cold <u>as</u> ice.*
The seven penguins were *<u>like</u> princesses.*
Flash was *fast <u>as</u> lightning.*
Larry was *cool <u>as</u> a cucumber.*

TELL ME MORE!

Similes help readers to understand and remember better what, exactly, an author is talking about. They help us form pictures in our minds. Here is a simile from the Bible: "Like a club or a sword or a sharp arrow is the man who gives false testimony against his neighbor" (Proverbs 25:18). Clearly, Solomon wanted to compare a man's false testimony to a club, a sword, or a sharp arrow. A man who makes such a testimony is using a deadly weapon! Besides helping us to "see" what they are talking about, people use similes to cause those who hear them to *think more deeply* than if they spoke in a simpler manner. For instance, do you think you would pay as close attention or think as deeply about Solomon's message if he had simply said, "A man who gives false testimony against his neighbor hurts his neighbor"?

When using similes, you also have to think about connotation, or what kind of feeling the word gives you. If you were trying to describe your dad's new car, you might say it is "red as a cherry" or "red like an apple." The words *cherry* and *apple* have pleasant connotations, and that pleasant feeling carries over to the car. You probably wouldn't say the car is "red as blood." The word *blood* gives a very different feeling and conjures up images of danger and injury. When you think about a new car, you don't want to think about blood. It just doesn't fit the mood. Make sure your similes fit the feeling you are trying to give.

Similes are frequently used in advertising. Chevrolet, for example, uses a simile when they say their trucks are "*like a rock*™." This marketing campaign seeks to convince you that their trucks are strong, sturdy, and dependable. They compare their trucks to rocks not because the trucks are made out of sandstone or quartz but because the trucks have rock-like qualities. A similar example is when State Farm Insurance boasts, "*Like* a good neighbor, State Farm is there." They want you to think that their company is reliable and friendly in the same way a good neighbor is.

Simple Predicate (see Predicate)

Simple Sentence

A simple sentence is a sentence comprised of a single independent clause, though it may have a compound subject and/or a compound predicate. A simple sentence can have one or more phrases, but it cannot have any dependent clauses.

Ex. The porcupine danced.
The porcupine and the skunk danced.
The skunk danced and sang with the porcupine.

Simple Subject (see Subject)

Singular

Singular means there is one of something.

Ex. The singular form of geese is goose.

Slang

Slang is the nonstandard vocabulary of a particular group or subculture, consisting usually of colorful figures of speech. Often used in fiction or personal writing, slang should be avoided in formal writing.

Ex. Phil needs to *seriously chill out*. (Phil really needs to relax.)

Michael couldn't believe his *homey* had *ratted him out* to the *fuzz*. (Michael couldn't believe his friend had turned him over to the police.)

Slash (see Diagonal)

Subject

The subject, which is always a noun or pronoun, is what a clause is about. Every clause has a subject. Subjects come in three varieties: simple, compound, and complete.

Ex. A **simple subject** is the noun or pronoun by itself. (Most *apprentices* obey their masters.)

A **compound subject** includes two or more simple subjects. (*Ben* and *Jerry* make ice cream.)

A **complete subject** includes not only a simple or compound subject, but also any words that modify or describe the subject—including adjectives, adverbs, and articles. (Most *young apprentices* are careful to obey their masters.)

TELL ME MORE!
Implied (or understood) Subject: You may occasionally notice that a sentence is missing a subject, yet it still makes sense! Why? Such sentences have implied (or understood) subjects. The implied subject is understood by the reader, even though it is not stated. You will often find implied (or understood) subjects in sentences expressing a command.

Ex. Go to your room! (The subject of the sentence, *you*, is implied [or understood].)

Delayed Subject: Cleft sentences contain delayed subjects. The true subject of a cleft sentence is not *there* or *it*; the true subject—if there is one—is whatever noun follows the verb. See also *Cleft Sentence*.

Ex. It was *Michael* who came up with the new lunch plan. (*It* is not the subject of this cleft sentence; *Michael* is the delayed subject. *It* is an expletive. See also *Expletive*.)

Subject-Verb Agreement

All nouns (or subjects) have two forms. They can be either singular (one) or plural (more than one). Verbs also have two forms: one form for singular subjects and another for plural subjects. The verb must be in agreement with the subject (noun or pronoun).

Ex. The *girl* writes. The *girls write*.
The *dog eats* quickly. The *dogs eat quickly*.
My *mom loves* to cook. My *parents love* to cook.

Subjects and verbs must also agree in *person*. Subjects (nouns and pronouns) occur in first, second, and third person. First person refers to one's self or one's own group. The first-person pronouns are *I* (singular) and *we* (plural). Second person refers to the person or group to whom you are speaking. The second-person pronoun is *you* (for both singular and plural).

When you are referring to someone or something that is neither first nor second person—"those people over there" or "that thing"—you are speaking in the third person. There are many pronouns for the third person. Correct usage of third-person pronouns depends on three things: (1) the number and gender of the thing you're talking about; (2) whether what you're talking about is a person or thing; and (3) whether it is the subject or the object of your conversation. The following chart summarizes correct third-person pronoun usage:

Gender	Subject/Object	Singular	Plural
Male	subject	he	they
	object	him	them
Female	subject	she	they
	object	her	them
Neuter (thing)	subject	it	they
	object	it	them

TELL ME MORE!
There are two cases where it is difficult to determine subject-verb agreement: when using a collective noun and when using proper names that include a plural noun.

Collective nouns always take singular verbs.

Ex. The word *family* is considered a collective noun because a *family* consists of more than one individual in *one group*. When you talk about your family, you say that it includes more than one person. The word *includes* is a verb in its singular form. The plural form of the same verb doesn't even sound correct. (Your family *include* more than one person). If you feel that you must use a plural verb, then speak of the members of the collective noun (Your family *members* include . . .).

Proper names that include a plural noun also take singular verbs (like *The Discoverers*—a book by Daniel Boorstin). In these instances, the entire name is a proper noun, and it is a proper noun representing a single thing.

Ex. *The Discoverers* is a great book. (NOT *The Discoverers* are a great book.)

Be careful to make sure that your nouns and pronouns don't flip back and forth between singular and plural and between first, second, and third person.

Ex. A person came into a store to buy some bubblegum, but then they forgot what they wanted. (This sentence started with a singular third-person subject ["a person"], but quickly shifted to a plural third-person subject ["they"]. This is a very common error!)

Subordinate Clause

A subordinate (or **dependent**) clause contains a subject and a predicate but does not convey a complete thought and/or cannot stand alone as a sentence. It is subordinate to—*depends on*—a separate, independent clause to "hold it up." Subordinate clauses begin with subordinating conjunctions and do not convey complete thoughts because of the subordinating conjunctions. See also *Subordinating Conjunction*.

Ex. Although everyone else wanted to eat Italian food

Because eagles are an endangered species

Subordinating Conjunction

A subordinating conjunction connects two clauses such that one of the clauses depends on the other to make sense. In other words, subordinating conjunctions place one clause under—subordinate to—the other, making it dependent on the other. Subordinating conjunctions always come at the beginning of a subordinate or dependent clause. See also *Subordinate Clause*.

Ex. Joe ran *when* he saw the bear. –or- *When* he saw the bear, Joe ran. (In both of these cases, *when* is the subordinating conjunction. We have to know that *Joe* ran before the clause *when he saw the bear* makes much sense.)

NOTE: The following is a list of some subordinating conjunctions: after, because, so that, when, although, before, that, where, as, if, though, whereas, in order that, till, while, as long as, provided that, unless, as though, since, and until.

Suffix

A suffix is a part added to a root word after the root to change its meaning.

Ex.   *Book* is a root word. If you add the suffix -s to it, it becomes books. What happened? Adding the suffix *-s* changes the meaning from singular to plural. Similarly, adding the suffix *-ed* to the end of the root word *want* changes it from present tense to past tense (*wanted*).

Syllable/Syllabication Rule

A syllable is a small unit of speech made up of a single, uninterrupted sound. Words may have one or many syllables.

Ex.   jump (one syllable—*jump*)

jumping (two syllables—*jump-ing*)

anesthesiologist (seven syllables—*an-es-the-si-ol-o-gist*)

TELL ME MORE!

The main reason to study syllables is learn to break words when they need to be broken. Syllables are the smallest parts of words that you are allowed to print on one line. If you need to break a word, you should write all the syllables you can on the first line, place a hyphen at the end of the line, and then finish the word on the line that follows.

Ex.   A common break point between syllables is between two consonants that are between two vowels (vc/cv—with *v* indicating vowels, *c* consonants). The syllables in the word picnic, for example, break between the consonants *c* and *n*, which are, in turn, between two vowels—*i* and *i*, respectively (pic/nic).

Synonym

Synonyms are words that have the same (or nearly the same) meaning.

Ex.   *big—large*
little—small

Tense (see Verb Tense)

Topic Sentence

A topic sentence introduces the subject of a paragraph. Topic sentences let the reader know what the paragraph will discuss. A topic sentence is usually found at the beginning of each new paragraph. Not all paragraphs have topic sentences, but they should be used in every persuasive paragraph and every paragraph of a formal essay.

Ex.   In first grade, Seth learned some of the harsh realities of life.

More people should know how to administer first aid.

Michael and I are not strangers.

TELL ME MORE!

A topic sentence introduces the subject of a paragraph, but it doesn't necessarily knock you over the head and scream *this is what this paragraph is about!* Instead, it whispers what the paragraph is about; it gives you hints. Using the sentences above, think about the paragraphs they introduce.

In first grade, Seth learned some of the harsh realities of life. What is this paragraph going to be about? What would you expect to find within it? You would probably expect to find a list of lessons about life that Seth learned in first grade. Maybe it will contain some stories about the circumstances and experiences by which he learned his lessons.

More people should know how to administer first aid. This paragraph probably has to do with first aid, why it is important, and/or the reasons why more people should learn how to administer it.

Michael and I are not strangers. This paragraph is probably meant to demonstrate how and why the author and Michael are not strangers. Put another way: it should tell how and why the author knows Michael.

Transitive Verb

A transitive verb is a verb that requires two nouns: (1) the subject to do the action; and (2) the object to receive the action or to be acted upon. Transitive verbs transfer action from one noun to another.

Ex.   Noah (subject) *pushed* the zebras (object) into the ark.

Ed *read*. (But what did Ed read? The label on a carton of milk? The newspaper? The Bible? You need to know *who* did the reading and *what* was read.)

Marie *baked*. (If someone told you that Marie baked, you would want to know *what* Marie baked. A cake? A pie? Cookies? The transitive verb *bake* requires a direct object.)

Understood Subject (see Subject)

Verb

A verb is a word that tells what someone or something *did*, *does*, or *will do*, or about what it was, is, or will be. The two types of verbs are action verbs and being verbs.

Action verbs express actions. When an action verb is used, it is possible to write a sentence using only two words.

Ex.   jump, talk, laugh, smile, shout

Sue jumps. (Which word is the noun? [*Sue*] Which is the verb? [*jumps*] *Jumps* tells what Sue is doing—it represents an action.)

Being verbs express states of being using the verb *to be*. They require at least three words, and the third word in a being-verb sentence is not a verb. The verb *to be* (in all its forms) links subjects with various characteristics. *To be* shows a logical connection between the subject and a noun or an adjective. In this way, a being verb clarifies the subject.

Ex.   Margaret *is* a teacher.
Zelda *is* angry.
The celery *is* green.
Bunny rabbits *are* fluffy.

The following chart summarizes the proper uses of the verb *to be*:

I *had been*	
we/you/they *had been*	**Past Perfect (Complete)**
he/she/it *had been*	
I *was*	
we/you/they *were*	Past
he/she/it *was*	
I have *been*	
we/you/they *have been*	**Past Progressive (Continuing)**
he/she/it *has been*	
I *am*	
we/you/they *are*	**Present**
he/she/it *is*	
I *will be*	
we/you/they *will be*	**Future**
he/she/it *will be*	

TELL ME MORE!

If you find that many of your sentences include some form of the verb to be, you can be sure you're writing in the passive voice. Replace as many to be's as you can with other, more active verbs!

For more information about specific types of verbs, see also *Helping Verb, Intransitive Verb, Linking Verb, Phrasal Verb,* or *Transitive Verb.*

Verb Tense

A verb's **tense** tells you when an action took, takes, or will take place—in the **past**, **present**, or **future**. We can speak of actions taking place in any one of a dozen or more tenses.

Ex.   **Simple** (the action simply happens):
- The *simple* past: The man walked.
- The *simple* present: The man walks.
- The *simple* future: The man will walk.

Continuing (the action keeps happening over a period of time):
- The *continuing* past: The man was walking.
- The *continuing* present: The man is walking.
- The *continuing* future: The man will be walking.

Perfect:
- The *past* perfect (the action ends prior to another past action): The man had walked.
- The *present* perfect (the action started in the past but continues or is completed in the present): The man has walked.
- The *future* perfect (the action will begin and will be completed by a specific time in the future): The man will have walked.

NOTE: Many tenses require more than just some form of the root verb; they require helping or auxiliary verbs.

If you put together a list that shows various tenses of a single verb, the list is called a conjugation. To conjugate a verb means to show its different forms, based on tense. Here is a sample conjugation of the verb *walk*:

he had walked	before sometime in the past
he had been walking	while something else was happening sometime in the past
he walked	sometime in the past
he was walking	for a period of time in the past
he has walked	before now

he walks	now
he is walking	for some period of time right now
he will have walked	after now but before sometime in the future
he will have been walking	for some period of time after now but before sometime in the future
he will walk	sometime in the future
he will be walking	for a period of time in the future

Vocalized Sounds

A vocalized sound is created when you say a word and/or create sound by using your vocal chords. You can tell if a sound is vocalized by placing your fingertips on your throat.

Ex.   Say the /m/ sound. Can you feel the vibrations? Those indicate you are vocalizing. Sometimes the suffix *-ed* is vocalized (it sounds like /d/—as in played).

Voice

Voice is a term used to describe whether the subject of a sentence is acting (active voice) or being acted upon (passive voice). **Active-voice** sentences always tell you who did the action. The subject comes first, and the subject does the action.

Ex.   The gardener mowed the grass.
Students will memorize words.

In **passive-voice** sentences, the subject of the sentence is acted upon, but does not act. The subject of the sentence is the object of the verb.

Ex.   The grass was mowed.
Words will be memorized by students.

TELL ME MORE!

If a sentence doesn't tell you who is doing the action, it must be a passive sentence.

Ex.   The stones were picked up. (by whom?)

To make a passive sentence active, you must not only provide information about who does the action, but you must make sure that you have the subject do the action!

Ex.   The stones were picked up by Sally. (passive—The stones [subject] are still the object of the verb, although we do now know that Sally was the one who picked them up.)

Sally picked up the stones. (active—Sally [subject] is responsible for the action.)

If you add the suffix *-ing* to a verb, it becomes a noun or an adjective. If it is used as a noun, it is called a *gerund*. If it is used as an adjective, it is called a *participle*. Participles and gerunds are good indicators of passive-voice sentences. When you use participles and gerunds, your sentences lose the strength they would have if you were to use your verbs as true verbs. Avoid participles and gerunds whenever possible!

To write well, use a lot of active-voice sentences. It's not necessary to avoid all passive-voice sentences, but keep in mind that the passive voice is deadly, dull, and weak. When subjects don't do anything, it slows things down and weakens the meaning. ■

This page intentionally left blank.

Grammar 5 Skills Matrix

How to Use the Skills Matrix

The next four pages contain the Grammar 5 Skills Matrix. Please consider each pair of facing pages one complete table that lists the skills used in either the first half or the second half of this program. Here's how to read the Skills Matrix:

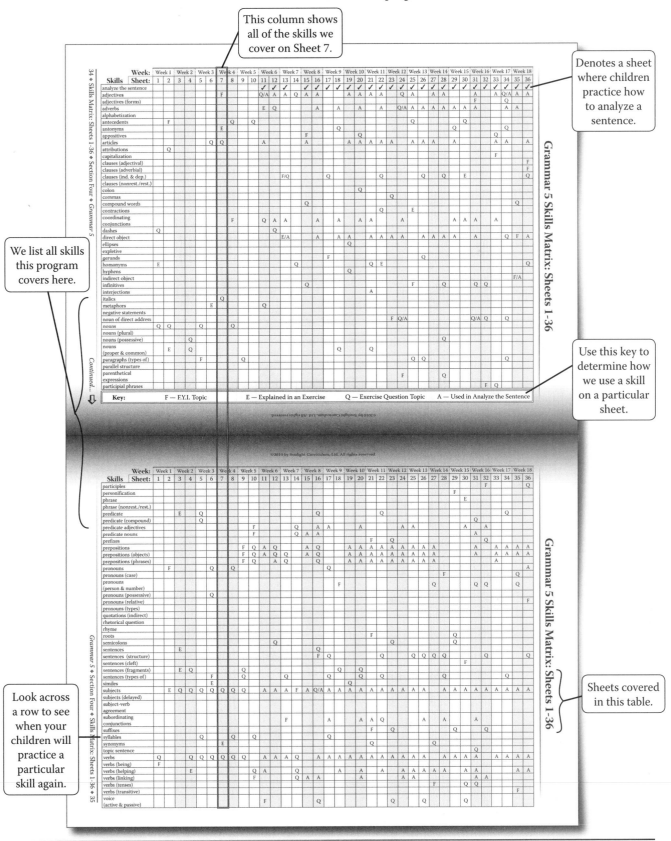

This column shows all of the skills we cover on Sheet 7.

Denotes a sheet where children practice how to analyze a sentence.

We list all skills this program covers here.

Use this key to determine how we use a skill on a particular sheet.

Look across a row to see when your children will practice a particular skill again.

Sheets covered in this table.

Key: F — F.Y.I. Topic   E — Explained in an Exercise   Q — Exercise Question Topic   A — Used in Analyze the Sentence

Grammar 5 Skills Matrix: Sheets 1-36

Week:	Week 1		Week 2		Week 3		Week 4		Week 5		Week 6		Week 7		Week 8		Week 9		Week 10		Week 11		Week 12		Week 13		Week 14		Week 15		Week 16		Week 17		Week 18	
Skills \ Sheet:	1	2	3	4	5	6	7	8	9	10	11	12	13	14	15	16	17	18	19	20	21	22	23	24	25	26	27	28	29	30	31	32	33	34	35	36
analyze the sentence											✓	✓	✓		✓	✓	✓	✓	✓	✓	✓	✓	✓	✓	✓	✓	✓	✓	✓	✓	✓	✓			✓	✓
adjectives											Q/A	A	A	Q	A	A			A	A	A	A	A	Q	A	A	A	A	A	A	A		A	Q/A	A	
adjectives (forms)							F				E	Q/A			F																F		Q			
adverbs											E	Q/A				A		A	A	A	A	A	Q/A	A	A		A	A	A		A		A	A	A	
alphabetization																																				
antecedents	F						E	Q										Q					Q	Q					Q	Q						
antonyms									Q	Q																								Q		
appositives					Q	Q																											Q			
articles			Q	Q							A				A				A	A	A	A	A		A	A	A		A				A	A	A	A
attributions	Q																																F			
capitalization																				Q																
clauses (adjectival)																																				
clauses (adverbial)																														E						
clauses (ind. & dep.)												Q	F/Q				Q				Q			Q		Q		Q							Q	
clauses (nonrest./rest.)																																				
colons																		Q		Q		Q					Q									
commas																						Q														
compound words															F	Q								E						Q					Q	
contractions																						Q														
coordinating conjunctions								F			Q	A	A	Q		A	A	A	A	A	A	A	A	A	A	A	A	A	A	A	A		A		A	
dashes			Q																																	
direct objects											Q		E/A		Q		Q	Q	Q																F	
ellipses																																				
expletives																	F																			
gerunds											Q			Q	Q			Q	Q	Q	Q	Q		A	E	Q			A	A			A		Q	
homonym/-phone/-graph	E										E						F				E															
hyphens																																		F/A		
indirect objects															Q							Q		F	F	A		Q			Q	Q				
infinitives									Q											A																
interjections																																				
italics																																				
metaphors																	Q	Q				Q												Q		
negative statements																																				
noun of direct address																							F	Q/A							Q/A	Q				
nouns	Q	Q																																		
nouns (plural)					Q			Q																												
nouns (possessive)		Q							Q													Q				Q								Q		
nouns (proper & common)	E		Q																																	
paragraphs (types of)					F																			F	Q	Q		Q								
parallel structure																																				
parenthetical expressions																																F	F		F	Q
participial phrases																																				

Key:
F — F.Y.I. Topic   E — Explained in an Exercise   Q — Exercise Question Topic   A — Used in Analyze the Sentence

Grammar 5 Skills Matrix: Sheets 1-36

Skills \ Sheet	1	2	3	4	5	6	7	8	9	10	11	12	13	14	15	16	17	18	19	20	21	22	23	24	25	26	27	28	29	30	31	32	33	34	35	36
participles																																				Q
personification																															F					
phrase																												F		E						
phrase (nonrest./rest.)			E																																	
predicates			E		Q											Q																		Q		
predicates (compound)					Q						Q											Q									Q					
predicate adjectives									F						A	A	A			A				A	A					A		A				
predicate nouns									F						A	A							Q	A							A					
prefixes																					F		Q						F			Q				
prepositions									F		A	Q	Q		A	Q	A		A	Q/A	Q/AQ/A	A	A	Q/A	A		Q/AQ/A				A		A		A	Q/A
prepositions (objects)									F		A	Q	Q		A	Q	A		A	Q/AQ/A	Q/AQ/A	A	A	Q/A	A		Q/AQ/A				A		A		A	Q/A
prepositional phrases									F		A	Q/A	Q		A	Q			Q	Q	Q	A	A	Q	Q	Q	Q						A			Q
pronouns	F					Q		Q						Q				Q																		
pronouns (case)				Q													Q																		Q	
pronouns (person & number)						Q			F									F								Q										
pronouns (possessive)																												Q								
pronouns (relative)																																				
pronouns (types)																																				
quotations (indirect)																																				
rhetorical questions																																				
rhyme																																				
roots											F		Q															Q	Q							
semicolons			E							Q		Q				Q						Q							Q							
sentences				Q			Q	Q			A	A	A	Q	A	F	Q		Q	Q	Q	Q	Q	Q	Q	Q	Q	Q	Q		Q	Q		Q		Q
sentences (structure)																														F						
sentences (cleft)																																				
sentences (fragments)				E					Q	Q					Q		Q		Q	Q				Q				Q	Q							
sentences (types of)					F	E			Q	F				Q	A									Q												
similes														F	A	Q/A			Q																	
subjects	E	Q	Q	Q	Q	Q	Q	Q	Q		A	A	Q/A	F	A	Q/A	A	A	A	A	A	A	A	A	A	A	A	A	A	A	A	A	A	A	A	A
subjects (delayed)																														F						
subject-verb agreement																																				
subordinating conjunctions																	A			A	A	A		A	A	A				A			A		A	
suffixes						F								F							F		F				F								F	
syllables										F							Q				Q					Q			Q		Q				Q	
synonyms																																				
topic sentences																																				
verbs	Q			Q	Q		Q	Q			A	A	A	Q	A	A	A	A	A	A	A	A	A	A	A	A	A	A	A	A	A	A	A	A	A	A
verbs (being)	F			E																	F		Q													
verbs (helping)				E					F/Q	F	A	A	Q	Q		A		A		A		A		A	A					A	A	A	A		A	A
verbs (linking)																A				A				A	A						A	A	A	A	A	A
verbs (tenses)																															Q				Q	
verbs (transitive)																					F		F		Q		F								F	F
voice (active & passive)													Q			Q						Q			Q	Q				Q						

Grammar 5 Skills Matrix: Sheets 37-72

Skills \ Week	19	19	20	20	21	21	22	22	23	23	24	24	25	25	26	26	27	27	28	28	29	29	30	30	31	31	32	32	33	33	34	34	35	35	36	36
Sheet	37	38	39	40	41	42	43	44	45	46	47	48	49	50	51	52	53	54	55	56	57	58	59	60	61	62	63	64	65	66	67	68	69	70	71	72
analyze the sentence	✓	✓	✓	✓	✓	✓	✓	✓	✓	✓	✓	✓	✓	✓	✓	✓	✓	✓	✓	✓	✓	✓	✓	✓	✓	✓	✓	✓	✓	✓	✓	✓	✓	✓	✓	✓
adjectives	Q	A	A	A	A	A	A	A	A	A	A	A	A/Q	A	A	A	A	A	A	A	A	A	A/Q	A	A	A	A/Q	A	A	A	A	A	A	A	A	A
adjectives (forms)																											Q	A				A				
adverbs	A	A	A	A	A		A	A	Q		A		A	A		A		A		A			A				Q	Q			A	Q/A	A	Q/A	A	A
alphabetization																								F												
antecedents		Q														Q																				
antonyms																	Q																			
appositives	Q		Q	Q					Q	A					Q				Q																Q	Q
articles	A	A		A	A		A	A		A	A	A	A	A	A	A		A	A	A			A		A	A	A	A	A	A	A	A	A	A	A	A
attributions						Q										Q				F							Q							Q	Q	
capitalization					Q											Q				Q																
clauses (adjectival)																																				
clauses (adverbial)																																				
clauses (ind. & dep.)	Q		Q											Q	Q	Q								Q			Q	Q	Q		Q					
clauses (nonrest./rest.)																																				
colons	Q		Q					Q																						Q						
commas	Q		Q															A																		
compound words									F															Q	Q					Q						
contractions							Q												A		A															
coordinating conjunctions		A		A	A		Q/A	A		A	A		A	A		A		A		A			A		A			A	A		A		A			
dashes		A	Q					A				Q							A													A				
direct objects	A	A		A	A	A		A	A	A	A	A	A	A	A	A	A	A	A		A	A	A	A	A	A	A	A	A		A	A	A	A	A	A
ellipses									F																		Q			Q						
expletives																F/Q	Q	Q									Q/A	Q/A								
gerunds			Q					Q						Q	Q				Q		Q				Q	Q		Q					Q			
homonym/-phone/-graph							Q			Q									A		Q		A				Q/A	Q	Q				Q		Q	Q
hyphens					Q																											A				
indirect objects																				A					A							A				
infinitives		Q	Q			F										Q							Q	Q			Q		A						Q	
interjections		F														F/Q						F		Q/A									Q			
italics																							F					Q			Q					
metaphors			Q																						Q											
negative statements					F															A																
noun of direct address										Q										Q	Q						Q/A	Q				A	Q		Q	
nouns																								A	Q		A	A								
nouns (plural)	Q	Q											Q																							
nouns (possessive)		F/Q	Q	Q								Q						Q												Q		Q				
nouns (proper & common)																		Q	Q												Q	A		Q	Q	
paragraphs (types of)														F							Q															
parallel structure																													Q							
parenthetical expressions											Q							Q			Q					Q										
participial phrases								Q														Q/A	Q/A		Q											

Key: F — F.Y.I. Topic   E — Explained in an Exercise   Q — Exercise Question Topic   A — Used in Analyze the Sentence

Grammar 5 Skills Matrix: Sheets 37-72

Week:	19		20		21		22		23		24		25		26		27		28		29		30		31		32		33		34		35		36	
Skills / Sheet:	37	38	39	40	41	42	43	44	45	46	47	48	49	50	51	52	53	54	55	56	57	58	59	60	61	62	63	64	65	66	67	68	69	70	71	72
participles			Q				A				Q		Q					A	Q		Q	Q	A	A	A	A	A	Q	A	Q		Q			A	A
personification								Q/A										A								A									A	
phrase																																				
phrase (nonrest./rest.)						F			Q																											
predicates				Q					Q		Q																				A	Q				
predicates (compound)																																				
predicate adjectives		A		A			A	A		A								A		A			A	A	A	A		A			A		A	A	A	A
predicate nouns	A	A	A											A	A	A				A					A					A	A					
prefixes								Q	Q			Q				Q		Q	Q/A		Q					Q				A			Q		Q	
prepositions	A	A	Q	Q	Q	A	A	A	Q	A	A	A	A	A	A		A	A	Q/A	A	Q	Q/A	A	A	Q/A	A	A	A	A	A	A	A	Q/A	A	Q/A	A
prepositions (objects)	A	A	Q	Q	Q	A	A	A	Q	A	A	A	A	A	A		A	A	Q/A	A	Q	Q/A	A	A	Q/A	A	A	A	A	A	A	A	Q/A	A	Q/A	A
prepositional phrases	Q	Q	Q	Q	Q		Q		Q										Q/A		Q	A	A	A	Q/A	Q				A	A		Q		Q	
pronouns																																				
pronouns (case)	Q															Q																				
pronouns (person & number)						Q	Q						Q										Q		Q								Q			
pronouns (possessive)	F		F	Q						Q																				Q	Q					
pronouns (relative)																	Q						Q							Q						
pronouns (types)												F	F																							
quotations (indirect)	E							Q																							Q					
rhetorical questions																													Q							
rhyme																							A	Q												
roots			Q	Q			Q			Q					Q			Q			Q		Q													
semicolons				Q		Q	Q		Q		Q	Q		A	Q			A		Q			Q	A	A	A	Q	Q	Q		Q	Q			Q	Q
sentences									E																											
sentences (structure)	Q					Q	Q	Q	Q		Q		A		Q			A	A		Q		A	A	A	A	A	A	A	A	A	A	A	A	A	A
sentences (cleft)													A	A	A		Q	A	A				A	A				A	A		A	A	A	Q	A	A
sentences (fragments)																																				
sentences (types of)		A		Q			Q				F	A	A	A										A										Q		
similes													A		A							A											Q			
subjects	A	A	A	Q/A	A	A	A	A	A	A	A	Q/A	A	A	A	A	A	A	A	A	A	A	A	A	A	A	A	A	A	A	A	A	A	A	A	A
subjects (delayed)																	Q																			
subject-verb agreement						Q										Q																				
subordinating conjunctions		A						A				A		A				A						A				A								
suffixes				Q			Q	A	Q						Q			Q	A	Q	Q										Q	Q				
syllables			Q			Q						Q	Q		Q								A	Q					Q				Q			
synonyms	Q																																			
topic sentences	F						Q										Q									Q										
verbs	A	A	A	A	A	A	A	A	A	A	A	A	A	A	A	A	A	A	A	A	A	A	A	A	A	A	A	A	A	A	A	A	A	A	A	A
verbs (being)	A	A	A		A			A			A		A		A		A	A	A		A		A	A	A	A	A	A	A	A	A	A	A	A	A	A
verbs (helping)	A									A					A			A	A	A			A				Q	Q	A	A	A	A	A	A	Q	A
verbs (linking)	A	A	A	A	A			A			A		A		A		A	A	A		A		A		A		A	A	A		A		A	A	A	A
verbs (tenses)	Q				Q		Q		Q		Q		Q	Q	Q		Q		A	Q	Q		A	A				Q	Q		A	Q	Q		Q	Q
verbs (transitive)																																				
voice (active & passive)							Q								Q										Q				Q							

This page intentionally left blank.

Bibliography

Applegate, Cathy. *Red Sand, Blue Sky*. Australia: McPherson's Printing Group, 1997. First published 1995 by Margaret Hamilton Books Pty Ltd. Page references are to the 1997 edition.

Buck, Pearl. *The Big Wave*. New York: HarperCollins Publishers, Ltd., 1986. First published 1947 by the Curtis Publishing Company. Page references are to the 1986 edition.

Burnford, Sheila. *The Incredible Journey*. New York: Bantam Doubleday Dell Books for Young Readers, 1996. Condensation appeared in *McCalls* magazine in March, 1961. Page references are to the 1996 edition.

Coatsworth, Elizabeth. *The Cat Who Went to Heaven*. New York: Aladdin Paperbacks, 2008. First published 1930 by Simon & Schuster, Inc. Page references are to the 2008 edition.

Coerr, Eleanor. *Sadako and the Thousand Paper Cranes*. New York: Puffin Books, 2004. First published 1977 by G.P. Putnam's Sons. Page references are to the 2004 edition.

Crofford, Emily. *Born in the Year of Courage*. Minneapolis: Carolrhoda Books, Inc., 1991.

Davidson, Margaret. *Louis Braille*. New York: Scholastic, Inc., 1971.

Fritz, Jean. *Homesick*. New York: Penguin Putnam Books for Young Readers, 1999. First published 1982 by G.P. Putnam's Sons. Page references are to the 1999 edition.

George, Jean Craighead. *Water Sky*. New York: HarperCollins Publishers, Ltd., 1987.

Grover, Wayne. *Ali and the Golden Eagle*. Littleton: Sonlight Curriculum, Ltd., 1997. First published 1993 by William Morrow & Company, Inc. Page references are to the 1997 edition.

Henry, Marguerite. *King of the Wind*. New York: Aladdin Paperbacks, 1991.

Kipling, Rudyard. *Just So Stories*. London: Puffin Books, 2008. Reissued with an introduction by Jonathan Stroud. First published 1902. Page references are to the 2008 edition.

North, Sterling. *Rascal*. New York: Puffin Books, 1990. First published 1963 by E.P. Dutton, a division of Penguin Books USA Inc.. Page references are to the 1990 edition.

Park, Linda Sue. *The Kite Fighters*. New York: Dell Yearling Books, 2002.

Polland, Madeleine. *Mission to Cathay*. Littleton: Sonlight Curriculum, Ltd., 1997. First published 1965. Page references are to the 1997 edition.

Robertson, Keith. *Henry Reed*. New York: Puffin Books, 1989. First published in the U.S. by Viking Penguin, 1958. Page references are to the 1989 Puffin edition.

Sperry, Armstrong. *Call it Courage*. New York: Aladdin Paperbacks, 1990. First published 1940 by Simon & Schuster, Inc. Page references are to the 1990 edition.

St. John, Patrticia. *Star of Light*. First edition. Chicago: Moody Press, 1953-06.

Thompson, Phyllis. *God's Adventurer: Hudson Taylor*. Singapore: Overseas Missionary Fellowship (IHQ) Ltd., 1997. First published 1954 by China Inland Mission. Page references are to the 1997 edition.

Treffinger, Carolyn. *Li Lun, Lad of Courage*. New York: Walker Publishing Company, Inc., 1995. First published 1947 by Abingdon-Cokesbury Press. Page references are to the 1995 edition.

Verne, Jules. *Around the World in Eighty Days*. Translated by Edward Roth. New York: Scholastic Inc., 1990. First published 1874. Page references are to the 1990 edition.

This page intentionally left blank.

My Notes

My Notes

My Notes

My Notes

My Notes

My Notes